London Decameron
Part 2

Production and publication:
BoD - Books on Demand, Norderstedt
Copyright: 2019 Karl Heinz Landenberger
ISBN 978-3-7494-5471-6

Interim conclusions of the
publisher

Several months have passed since the release of the first part of London Decameron, which covers days one to five, and the publication of the second part, covering days six, seven, and eight. Enough time to draw some interim conclusions. We can look at reader reactions in conversations and in reader letters about London Decameron. The diversity of the judgments on these London stories, depending on the interest of the reader, is surprising to behold.

Scapa Flow

A reader who had just made a trip to the Orkney Islands informed me that the statement that it is home to the biggest ship graveyard is not entirely correct. For a sum of 40,000 dollars, an American entrepreneur is said to have received permission to lift and scrap the shipwrecks. The monetary value of the proud imperial fleet was thus a mere 40,000 dollar.

Old postcard

He had attached an old postcard to the email, showing the German battle fleet in its full glory one last time before the self-ordered sinking.

Trial records

A second attachment held copies of the trial documents against the commander who had unilaterally ordered that these proud battleships simply be handed over to the English. Yet, he was now being convicted by the English.

Value in gold

A third addendum made the comment that defeated Germany had to pay out the value of the war fleet, but in German Goldmarks: in other words, the astronomical war reparations included several Goldmarks.

Literature in the digital age

These reader letters indicate something very interesting. The additional information they provide enriches the original literary text. A way of making this information instantly available to any future reader needs to be found. You could put novels and stories online so that anybody could add a link to the individual chapters or sections, allowing a potential reader to click on them if they so wished.

Incorrect date

An engineer from Heckler & Koch, the company that succeeded Mauser Werke, felt moved to share that Churchill received his Mauser pistol for his 21st birthday, rather than at 18. The pistol carries the designation G96 because it was, in 1896, the world's first self-loading automatic pistol on the market. Churchill was born in 1875, so by 1896, when his mother purchased the latest model for him, he would have already been 21 years old. This amendment is interesting and deserves to be recorded.

Anarchists

A highly noteworthy letter also disclosed that the last section in the story was contradicted by the raid on Sydney Street. They were by no means harmless hoodlums, but in fact belonged to a group of anarchists who had fled to London as refugees following the failed revolution in Russia in 1905.

Out in force

The deployment of 200 specially trained police officers by Scotland Yard indicates that it really was a major operation. The bandits had Mauser semi-automatic weapons that outperformed the weapons of the forces, which subsequently led to the London police force being equipped with better, more modern weapons.

Refugees

These revolutionaries entered the country as refugees when the revolution and the planned murder of the Tsars in 1905 ended with the suppression of the uprising and the agitators being prosecuted. In London, they were received sympathetically, but this did not prevent them from supplementing their financial requirements with bank robberies and lootings.

Expropriation of the expropriators

This was their motto. They also wanted to introduce the concept of the classless society to England, but this was not met with approval on all sides. While influential circles in London certainly considered it desirable in Russia, they did not necessarily want to accept it in their own country. The support that Stalin, Lenin, and others, who lived in London for a while, could draw on declined noticeably over time, resulting in the revolutionaries seeking refuge in other cities. Lenin, for example, went to Zurich.

Belittlement

The trivialization of these anarchist acts of terrorism also applies to the Sydney Street raid. In the end, there was only talk of two harmless crooks, though it was obvious that a large group of Baltic anarchists were involved in the attack. Georg Gardstein and Max Schmoller, the only two who were found charred in the basement and whose ashes were swept up with a broom, had long been part of the group that had previously been involved in the Tottenham Outrage and the Hunditsch murder, where they had dug a tunnel through the wall into a jewelry store. Since then, however, there has been no sign of Peter Piatkow. He was one of the main ringleaders. It is likely that he was completely incinerated on an upper floor. The other participants – Jakob Vogel, Luba Milstein, Fritz Schwarz and Jakob Peters – were acquitted because their direct involvement could not be proven. It is a bit like today, when it is stated that a victim of violence – a person whose temple is struck with a shoe, as occurred in Chemnitz – actually died of pre-existing heart failure, rather than the resulting head injuries.

Humor

Other trivial stories also attracted interest and inspired readers to put pen to paper. The fact that Churchill spat out the dry and, for him, too sour Riesling at the renowned Hotel Dolder inspired a writer to consider the following. He could not believe that Churchill would have spat in his neighbor's plate on this occasion. But spitting on the floor would not have worked either, as he was sitting at the table after all. Spitting sideways was even less likely given the neighboring tables on every side. Spitting on the tablecloth would have been a real hassle at this large table. In order to clean up the damage, everything would have had to be cleared away. So, the only remaining possibility: Spitting into his own plate. The letter writer had made inquiries, but nowhere was it revealed where Churchill had spat. It remains a mystery, but perhaps he really did simply spit into his own glass. This grandiose idea was conveyed to me by my secretary Katrin.

Comparison

Nevertheless, the writer was also quick to offer a comparison. Hitler was invited to the Hanfstaengl family's home in Munich, a family with whom he was acquainted. It is well-known that he was a committed teetotaler. Mrs. Hanfstaengl succeeded, nonetheless, in persuading Hitler to try a small glass of a particularly outstanding Riesling. Anyone drinking wine or beer for the first time is unlikely to have a particularly pleasant first experience. This was also true in Hitler's case. He found the premium Riesling sour, but bravely gulped down the first sip. He then, however, asked Mrs. Hanfstaengl to bring him the sugar bowl. He sweetened what he called the "Sourling" with a heaped teaspoon of sugar. He did not want to be so rude as to leave the glass without drinking the wine.

Original idea

A friendly couple, well-traveled, though strangely never to London, were inspired by the narrative framework of my London stories and flew to London for a few days on a whim. Schedule: Proceed exactly as per the specifications of the short stories. Reading my book was the preparation. They even wanted to eat the same dishes at the restaurants described. So, on the first day, it's Hyde Park with fish and chips at The Swan. On the second day, the East End and The Tower with lamb and cherry tomatoes. On the third day, a Thames cruise, Westminster Abbey and Churchill's "War Rooms", followed by ratatouille at the French House in the evening. On the fourth day, it's an art gallery and the British Museum, then fish soup at Jaimie. The fifth day is St. Paul's and the City of London and, by necessity, burgers.

In the following book, covering the sixth, seventh, and eighth days, Hampton Court Palace forms the framework, alongside Windsor Castle and the Hampstead Heath.

Perhaps they are planning another three-day weekend in London.

Crete

Another family had seen the boneyards of German parachutists on their trip to Crete. They were particularly touched by the history of the parachutists. As long as they hung in the air, these were an ideal target for the enemy. Their equipment and rifles had to be discarded due to the weight on the special parachutes. This meant that when the soldiers landed, they were far from ready for action. They first had to search for their weapons, and the parachute they had sailed down on had often landed a long distance from their own landing site. This landing and the subsequent expulsion of the English military was only successful after the most monstrous losses; it borders on a miracle. It can be attributed entirely to the boundless heroism of the German soldiers.

Heroism

Heroism does need to be mentioned because, in addition to a British sea power that was entirely superior and 32,000 Brits on Crete itself, there were only 22,000 German paratroopers. Of these, more than 7,000 – one third – were shot down in the first hour. A paratrooper hanging in the air is an ideal target. It is almost unbelievable that the Germans managed to scare off the Brits in spite of this.

Churchill's fantasies

Despite the Germans' incomprehensible losses, England suffered a defeat which Churchill eventually had to take responsibility for as he had ordered the Greek adventure. He attributed the failure of the British to prevent the Germans from conquering Crete to an infamous deception by the

Germans. They are said to have parachuted in disguise as monks and nuns. For that reason, the English did not shoot at them. However, this lie quickly began to seem too unbelievable and he corrected himself, saying that they parachuted in wearing New Zealand uniforms. Therefore, the English initially believed them to be allies. This did sound a bit more believable, it's true.

In any case, I was equally pleased to receive this letter. In the age of digital communication, readers can also make contributions to a book and need not limit themselves to passive reading.

Astonishing

The chapter which I expected to attract the biggest feedback was not mentioned by a single reader. I'm talking about the chapter concerning the assassination in the Bürgerbräu beer hall in Munich. If the British intelligence services had not passed on the information to the Gestapo on Churchill's orders – that Elser would receive 4,000 Reichsmark in Zurich in preparation for an assassination – then Elser would probably not have been placed under surveillance. His planned assassination could have been successful, which is to say, he might have succeeded in killing Hitler. In the style of devotional literature, you could put it thus: Churchill saved Hitler's life. Who should be grateful to him for this noble gesture?

Minor corrections

The Spanish translator very conscientiously noted some minor discrepancies. To the Romans, Mare Nostrum meant the entire Mediterranean and not just the Adriatic Sea. The Nietzsche quotation: "Humans will decline, but humans are only a transition" is found not in The Antichrist, but in Zarathustra.

Additional amendments

The same translator also made the correction that Unity Mitford's grandfather did not carry out the translation, he merely wrote the foreword for it.

Jokes and witty sayings

Some, especially those by Churchill, are well represented. But there are, of course, many more. The "No sports" quote is among the most well-known. For one Churchill admirer, this saying was wide of the mark. However, he also noted straight away that this saying only has limited application. In his youth, Churchill is actually said to have been quite sporty. He was even one of the best at foil fencing at his school. His first political deployment took him to India. There, he was considered one of the best polo players, a sport that requires a high level of agility.

Poker

He was also a passionate player of poker. To celebrate the victory over Hitler, it was decided that a poker game with President Truman should crown the celebration. Remember, Truman was the successor to Roosevelt, who had died a few weeks before the end of the war. In this game Churchill lost one million pounds sterling to Truman in a single evening. It was the entire profit from his war bonds. In 1938 he had already lost his entire fortune once because war had not broken out. If Strakosch had not bailed him out, even his private home, Chartwell, would have been auctioned off. Despite this, he took the risk of buying war bonds again in 1939. This time, however, he was more cautious and bought smaller sums, but nonetheless they still yielded one million.

Younger generation

Something more general also struck me. Regarding the reception of the London stories, all of the events lie so far back in the past for the generation born after WW2 that they have almost no conception of them. They will never have heard the famous names of the politicians, war heroes and artists of that period. Nor do they interest them. These are today's 50-year-olds.

The youngest generation

They have forgotten how to read. A hypotactic sentence with attribution and subordination can no longer be logically processed. A series of several of these sentences clearly overwhelms their ability to concentrate. Today WhatsApp is used to speak and record. Almost nothing is typed anymore.

Audiobook

A solution for 20 to 30-year-olds might be the production of an audiobook. Black letters on white paper that translate into ideas require the training of brain functions that the schools of today no longer aspire to. For the even younger ones, even this is out of the question. For them, only transferring it into a comic series remains as an option.

Screen adaptation

The only serious alternative that remains is a good screen adaptation. That's what I wish for. Or for the stories to be brought to life in the theater.

Preview

In the next year there will be a final, third part of the London stories. This will cover the ninth and tenth days.

Addendum

Two letters have just been tossed into the mailbox, but I would still like to tell you what they say.

Deceiving Poland

The first writer is particularly interested in Churchill's deception of the Poles. First, the broken promise to intervene in the event of Poland being attacked. That did not happen after the attack by the Germans and certainly not after the attack by the Soviet Union. Finally, a few weeks before the end of the war, Churchill and the US withdrew all support from the government-in-exile, leaving Poland as a vassal state to Stalin as bounty.

Gibraltar plane crash

The worst thing of all, however, was the murder of Sikorski and his entire government staff in an ordered airplane crash in Gibraltar, in which the pilot was the only survivor. That's how the writer Hochhuth describes it, at least.

Hochhuth

He featured this tragedy in a play, "Soldiers", that received international attention. Because the pilot was still alive at that time, and he was portrayed as an accomplice to the plane crash, he was awarded compensation on the grounds of defamation by the courts. No proper evidence for Hochhuth's theory exists. The papers are still locked away because they concern official secrets.

Katyn

Katyn was the cause of this tragedy. Gaining ground on the Germans, they discovered the mass grave of Polish officers and intellectuals on April 13th, 1943. It was clear that the Soviets were responsible for this massacre. However, given that Churchill had collaborated with Stalin in the meantime, there were difficulties. Responsibility was shifted onto the Germans, but the Poles wanted a factually accurate investigation. They turned to the Red Cross. However, Churchill could not get into difficulties with Stalin. For that reason, he chose to sacrifice Sikorski and his Polish government-in-exile. The pilot went into the cockpit with his lifejacket on. The only eyewitness of the crash testified that the aircraft did not crash, but rather made a wheels-up landing. During the investigation neither the eyewitness nor the only surviving pilot, Edward Prchal, were questioned. A criminal investigation of the incident was excluded for reasons of secrecy.

The second letter

The writer points out that Churchill wanted to conceal the fact that it was he alone who wanted to force the abdication of Edward VIII. This was why he gave a speech in parliament in which he was the only one to speak out against the abdication of the king. His speech was booed, though it is not clear whether those booing had been initiated into the deception.

"Money rules the world"

Churchill's ordering party, which enforced the abdication, was actually Baron von Rothschild. He also tried to disguise this fact. He pointedly invited the King and Wallis Simpson to a grandiose dinner, during which he openly expressed his deep regret regarding Edward VIII's desire to abdicate. The King was smart enough to play along, although of course he knew exactly what was going on. But what use would a scandal have been if it had become public? He who has the money, and owns all of the newspapers, has more power than even the king. In principle everybody knows: "Money rules the world". Only then one would have also learned that the money also has a name and that its name is Rothschild.

One more correction

An acquaintance who is a history teacher pointed out that Houston fell for a piece of fake news: when he assumed that Franco's generals had refused to obey orders as a result of the extreme bribery. In reality, the reason is thought to have been a different one. Franco would have insisted that if he were to conquer Gibraltar, the mainland opposite, Morocco, where Spain has only two enclaves, Ceuta and Melilla, would have to be part of the area captured. This area was still, despite the surrender, answerable to the Vichy government. And Hitler definitely did not want to mess things up with them.

Amusing

I have not seen one of my closest acquaintances for a long time. He is extremely wrapped up in his job. Finally, last night, he stopped by for a brief visit. This was especially important to me because I knew he had purchased the London stories, and I wanted to know what he thought of them. "These stories are amusing", he said shortly after the greeting. I was especially happy about that, so I would like to add this remark as a last supplement to the reader's reactions. The author is particularly keen to provide stories that not only arouse interest, but that the reader also finds pleasure in reading. Schiller wrote down this contradiction in five words:

"Life is serious, art carefree."

The sixth day
Bus journey to Hampton Court (6.1)

Houston promised me something very special for this day, something that London visitors rarely get to see. Namely, the beautiful gardens surrounding Hampton Court Palace. Hampton Court is located up the Thames, quite far from the center on the outskirts of the city.

To get there, we took one of the London double decker buses, because we wanted to see London's neighborhoods on the way; these are more reminiscent of small towns, idyllic with their small front gardens and the typical houses for just one family.

Miroslav

During the journey he also told me that we were going to meet one of his best friends there, a person who is always part of the small group who gather for regular discussion evenings. His father came to London in 1941 with the Polish government-in-exile.

Flight of the Polish government

The government in Warsaw fled immediately after defeat by the Germans. Normally, a government stays and negotiates a peace treaty with the victors. In this case, the Poles would probably have had to agree to a connecting road and railway between Germany and East Prussia. The government officials, however, presumably assumed that Hitler would make short work of them and took themselves over the Romanian border to safety. The Romanians were allies of the Germans, and so they were interned there. This led to a new Polish government-in-exile being formed under Sikorski.

Polish government-in-exile

Sikorski had already been president once and was known to detest the Germans. He said: "We need to capture the homes and fields of the Germans" – meaning the Germans whose territory was awarded to the Poles following the First World War – "and if they do not run away themselves, we will have to kill them." These words of a statesman sound quite alarming from today's perspective. More than one million Germans were driven out in this way, straight after the end of the First World War, well before the outbreak of the Second World War. According to accounts from the Nazis, more than 65,000 Germans were also killed in massacres. Churchill, however, reduced this number. In his ten-volume history of the Second World War, he writes that the figure actually stood at 8,000 and was therefore not worth mentioning.

Temporary seat of government

Sikorski initially went into exile in Paris along with the members of his government. The disappointment with Churchill was too great. It was he who had pushed them to war, and who, in spite of a pact of assistance, had abandoned them so ignominiously. After the defeat of France, however, the exiled government had no choice but to go to England.

Hitler's concessions

Hitler had almost reached an agreement with Poland offering the Poles astonishing concessions, far greater than the Weimar government had ever agreed to.

Indeed, he had even planned to take action against the Bolsheviks together with the Poles. The middle and upper classes in Poland were opposed to a communist revolution, just like in Germany. For this, Poland was promised the whole of Lithuania, as in the Jagiellonian era. Areas in Ukraine where Poles resided, although in the minority, were also to be annexed to Poland.

Churchill's promises

Churchill, however, had promised the Poles vastly more than this if they did not cooperate with Hitler. They were to receive all of East Prussia, Silesia, and Mecklenburg-Vorpommern with the entire Baltic Sea coast. What's more, this is along with the Mark Brandenburg together with the capital of Berlin, which were particularly important to them for historical reasons. For people today, this is almost inconceivable. The Poles fell for these promises.

Cover-up

After the Second World War, however, Churchill acted as if the Poles had enforced the displacement of the Germans from their homeland entirely autocratically, against their wishes. In the Iron Curtain speech before American students at Fulton University, he even spoke of the injustice of the displacement. He knew exactly, therefore, that he had contravened international law and human rights, yet deemed it clever to cover it up.

"Brandenburg"

"Brandenburg" was the biggest stronghold of the then-Gentile West Slavic region. The Poles saw their ancestors in these tribes. It was for this reason that they reclaimed these branches for themselves. These branches were forced to convert to Christianity at the time of the Crusades, around 1200. The population, however, was not driven out. Over the centuries they mixed with the Germans and took up their language. The remnants of the Slavic languages are only retained in the Spreewald area and are spoken by Sorbs and Wends. But to this day, the family names in this area are proof that the majority of the population have Slavic roots. One million German surnames are of Polish origin. I thought of a story about that.

Thomas Gottschalk

He is a popular entertainer in the Federal Republic. He comes from this area. Curious as he is, he allowed his DNA to be analyzed and was completely astonished when the results showed that 50% of his genetic makeup is of Polish origin. For all intents and purposes, though, this is not really that surprising. The same result is likely for all those who originate from Brandenburg and Mecklenburg-Vorpommern, if I take your information as a starting point, dear Houston.

Shitstorm

Gottschalk made a harmless joke on that point. This surprising discovery about his "roots" inspired him to say, rather self-deprecatingly: "Now I know why I shoplifted so happily as a child."
It is after all well-known that Poles in border areas were particularly active in stealing cars. That this self-deprecating joke unleashed a shitstorm is, however, not a sign of a relaxed relationship and interaction.

Displacement

In principle, the Poles had also expropriated and driven out their own compatriots after 1945, though they had simply taken on the German language over the course of 800 years.

Ignorance

I admitted to Houston that I had only heard of this historic situation through him. I knew nothing about a lot of things. My impression is that German history is simply edited out of the syllabus in German schools.

Racial purity

In the horse and dog breeding spheres, purity of breeding is an imperative. Many believe that racial purity should also be of utmost importance in the human race. Hitler, for example, was convinced that the high level of intelligence among the Jews could be traced back to the fact that the Jews had attached great importance to racial purity throughout the entire course of their history. A Jew could be someone with a Jewish mother. The identity of the father didn't even come into it. Perhaps even the mothers were not entirely sure.

Coudenhove-Kalergi

The eminent politician Coudenhove-Kalergi, himself of mixed-race origin with the most extraordinary of abilities, was convinced that the mixing of races produced inferior subjects. His father was from ancient Bohemian nobility, which had mixed with Dutch bloodlines, while his mother was a Kalergi, a Japanese aristocrat woman.

Interbreeding

We are discussing this theory. It seemed more probable to me that miscegenation is in fact better than racial purity. Coudenhove-Kalergi is the best example of this. This is also hardly depicted anywhere better than in Saxony and Brandenburg, as we have already seen from the example of Thomas Gottschalk, where the 50–50 mixture of Germanic and Slavic is usual. The great geniuses: Bach, Handel, Schumann, and Nietzsche are most likely the result of the successful mixing two races. However, it would still be a shock if DNA analysis of Martin Luther were to show that this essential German was possibly genetically half-Polish.

Hitler–Stalin pact

Hitler was unable to carry out his plan to act in concert with the Poles against Bolshevism, as the Poles had promised the English that they would provoke Germany into war. This meant that Hitler had to change fronts and formed an alliance with Stalin. Hitler wanted to avoid a war on a second front, as had happened in the First World War, under all circumstances.

Fire and water

This was the most paradoxical alliance imaginable. Hitler's main aim was the destruction of Bolshevism. Stalin's end goal was the consummation of the international revolution, which could only be deemed successful once red flags were waving in Berlin. This is a quotation by Lenin.

In his pact with Stalin, he reassured the Bolsheviks that if they signed a non-aggression pact, they would be allowed to occupy the Baltic nations and the areas that the Poles had incorporated against international law in 1920, although only a minority of one million Poles had settled there compared to six million Belarusians and Ukrainians.

This was Churchill's promise to Stalin, were Hitler to attack – the minimum demand, so to speak. This abandonment of the Baltic states came easily to Churchill. He had no relationship at all to these countries and their histories. Hitler, on the other hand, knew how many Baltic Germans lived there and that the big cities like Riga and Reval (now known as Tallinn) had a broad Hanseatic history.

Double surprise

That the Hitler–Stalin Pact came into being attracted worldwide surprise. Albeit not for Churchill. His plan was to destroy not just Hitler, but Stalin too. He wanted to set the pair against each other so that they would destroy one another. For that to occur, however, a war had to break out and that was difficult, as Hitler knew that Germany was far from well-equipped for that after Versailles. He would never have attacked Poland had he not received the backing of Stalin.

Churchill reassured Stalin that if he were to agree the moratorium with Hitler, he would receive the full support of the British Empire and the United States. He would have the freedom to strike whenever he thought the time was best for Russia. He decided on this plan with the firm intention to break at a time that suited him.

Two-way

But of course, Hitler knew that Stalin would not adhere to this pact. He had no intention to either. He was, however, of the opinion that he could create facts that would lead to a turnaround in the global configuration of powers.

And so, the first shot was fired in Danzig. This started the Second World War. One of the first sacrifices was the massacre in Katyn.

Once Stalin learned through his secret service of the original plans against the global communist revolution he would lead, he took revenge. In the areas claimed by Poland, which had now fallen to him in the Hitler–Stalin Pact, he carried out purges, „liquidating" the Polish gentry and all high-ranking officers. However, these mass murders were only made public when the Germans discovered the mass graves at Katyn as they advanced.

Churchill's 1st betrayal

All of the promises Churchill had made to the Poles were untenable once the Polish army had been attacked by the Germans. The military assistance that had been promised to them failed to materialize. When the Russians marched into Poland, back-up remained unforthcoming. Churchill maintained that the alliance had only been valid against the Germans.

Churchill's 2nd betrayal

After the war, Churchill betrayed Poland again. Two weeks before the Potsdam Conference, he sent the Polish government-in-exile "home". Stalin had conquered the entire area of Poland and cooperation between the exiled government and Stalin was out of the question for both them and for Stalin, and not just as a result of Katyn. For this reason, the Polish government-in-exile remained in the West, but were increasingly recognized by fewer and fewer states, eventually receiving only the support of the Vatican. The Poles fighting so bravely did not want to return to their homeland either. The Stalinist dictatorship was worse for them than life in a foreign country. Large numbers of Polish soldiers who had crossed the channel during Operation Downfall (X-Day) and fought in the

Netherlands and northern Germany, remained and settled there.

Miroslav

Miroslav's father remained in England. He married an Englishwoman and Miroslav was born in London and grew up there. He brought his wife, however, back from Poland. She is a Polish woman from Krakow, named Mila.

Miroslav works as a tour guide. He mainly guides Polish groups who do not speak English around Hampton Court Palace.

We were going to take part in one of his tours, they are actually bilingual. Afterwards, we were invited to lunch with him and his wife, Mila.

Hampton Court Gardens (6.2)

First, though, we wanted to take a short walk through the splendid gardens. Houston walks there regularly. "The best thoughts come to me while walking. In general, nothing clever comes to me while sitting down, particularly at a desk. Yawning emptiness and white paper before me. After an hour, there are some crossings out and corrections, but barely a useable sentence. But here, my thoughts can wander."

Peripatetic

You are obviously a genuine Peripatetic, like in the time of Plato. His dialogues also came into being while walking and in discussion with his students.

Royal Private Garden

We started our circular walk in the Royal Private Garden south of the palace. From there, there is a view of the palace's imposing southern facade. Christopher Wren designed it. He also carried out the redesign of the original garden according to a French model. This is how a typical Baroque garden was formed with a round pond and parterres in geometric patterns.

Demolition

There was a plan to demolish the old palace entirely and to rebuild it in classical Baroque style. Thankfully, the money ran out. It would have been a real shame if the main palace of Henry VIII, where he lived with all of his six wives and his children, no longer existed. Houston confessed that his relationship to this palace is the most emotional for him.

Banks of the Thames

The path led us along the Thames where we admired a richly ornamented, wrought iron fence along its winding banks. Slightly to the west of this, we marveled at Mantegna's "Triumphs of Caesar" in the Orangery. "The Great Vine" is found in the greenhouse beside the Orangery. This grapevine is the biggest in the world, with a circumference of 3.8 m and up to 75 meters of vines.
Once a year, the biggest flower show in the world takes place here.

Fountain garden

East of this we strolled around the 12 fountains in the semi-circular fountain garden, richly decorated with statues. To the north is the "Wilderness", a garden with high, supported hedges and the big maze with 2-meter high yew hedges. This is where London's homosexuals meet. Not far from this, in a bend in the Thames, there is a large deer park with 270 animals.

Homosexuality (6.3)

For a long time, this was a taboo topic. Today marriage and building a family are rather the exception. The big question when it comes to homosexuality is: What did nature intend with the creation of homosexual tendencies? What evolutionary function does this phenomenon fulfil? Today the accepted theory goes like this: The most vigorous prevail reproductively and, as a result, a constant process of evolution takes place. Among animals, it is the strongest creatures that can breed and guarantee the protection of its offspring. And among humans? The most attractive man gets the prettiest wife!

Genetic defect

Homosexual couples have no offspring. The official belief is: These humans have a genetic defect and for that reason Mother Nature has ensured that they cannot reproduce. Do you believe this as well?

Examples

Houston had to laugh. This theory sounds logical, but look at the reality. The most wonderful and the best footballer Cristiano Ronaldo has volunteered that he is gay. "I'm gay, but I'm rich." Where's the genetic defect there? He is also a father of four. His eldest is a charming chap who looks very like his father and cuts a very bonny figure. In other world class footballers, a genetic defect is equally difficult to imagine. The most coveted actresses and singers – real womanizers – often turn out to be gay. Even Churchill was rumored to be gay.

Cadet

A cadet is assigned to a British officer as a bellhop. The father of the cadet assigned to Churchill filed a lawsuit against Churchill, because his son was completely destroyed by the sexual abuse. The father, however, withdrew this charge when he realized that he had no chance before the court against a person of such high standing.

Hitler and Hess

Even Hitler was rumored of having these sorts of relations with Hess. There is a view that alleges he persecuted homosexuals with such force in order to mask his own homosexuality.
The theory of a genetic defect, therefore, is not helpful.

§ 175

This paragraph made homosexual acts a punishable offense. In the Old Testament, they could even be punishable by death. The problem for fundamentalist Christians is that this command is no longer applied.

Zeus

Among the ancient Greeks, on the other hand, even the highest god, Zeus, had a pretty lad as a butler: Ganymede. Rembrandt paints this scene to show Ganymede being kidnapped by Zeus' eagle while still a small child. He paints this scene in an utterly human, all-too-human, way. In shock, something happens to the whining little boy... he wets himself.

Alexander the Great

He destroyed the Persian empire of Darius and expanded the spread of Greek culture all the way to the Indus. Roxanna was his favorite of his wives, but he also had a male best friend. At the height of his power, he was indulged like an oriental despot in Babylon. His bosom friend, however, did not want to kneel down before him. But as Alexander had had more than enough to drink, he lost control over his behavior and battered his best friend to death. He never recovered from this loss once he was sober again.

Achilles

The most glorious hero in Homer's epic about Troy shamefully defiled the body of Hector because he had killed one of his best friends, Patroclus, in battle. He is the ideal of a man, like Siegfried is to the Germans. In the case of Achilles, a genetic defect can also be excluded.

Be honest

Houston, you are so well versed in homosexuality that I have to assume that it's not just because of the beautiful gardens that you've been coming here all these years. You have met similarly minded people here.

Honestly answered

Let's just say this: I don't just like seeing Venus of Milo, I also like Apollo by Belvedere and Hermes by Praxiteles and the thorn-pulling boy by Polykleitos.

Alcibiades

He was Pericles' nephew, the greatest statesman of the period when Athens was experiencing its greatest cultural heyday. He was considered the most beautiful man in the city. As a young man, all of the women flocked to him, absenting themselves from their husbands. Once he was a man, all of the husbands walked out on their wives and headed in his direction.

Socrates

Even Socrates was thought to harbor a soft spot for him, which is hardly surprising when you consider that he was married to Xanthippe. She was so quarrelsome that her name became a byword for all malevolent and cantankerous wives – of which there are more than one might think.

Syracuse

Alcibiades became cocky with this level of adulation and went as far as vandalizing the Athenian *hermai* and waging the catastrophic military campaign against the wealthiest Greek city on Sicily, Syracuse.

Aristophanes

I have to tell you about a funny theory about the comic poet Aristophanes. You're certain to know his comedy Lysistrata. The women of Athens denied their husbands because they never had any time for them and were always away on military campaigns.

The spherical human being

This comic poet took the view that there are three types of humans: Those descended from the sun, those descended from the Earth, and those descended from the moon. All three types are spherical in shape, exactly like the deities from which they derived. All have four legs, four arms and two heads. They can walk in any direction and they were so powerful that the other gods were jealous.

Division

The most powerful god, Zeus, separated them for a reason: in order to halve their opportunities. But ever since then each one has been searching for the missing half that once belonged to them. Two men were formed from the one descended from the sun. Their creator is male: Helios (Greek) as well as Sol (Latin). (The German language is the only one in which the sun is female.)

Two women were formed from the one descended from the Earth. Gaia (Greek) or Terra (Latin) is a female deity.

A man and a woman were created from the one descended from the moon. Semele (Greek) and Luna (Latin) are inconsistent: at one point the full moon, then increasing or reducing to the new moon. As a consequence, their creations are also those with the lowest value.

The most valuable are the men descended from the sun. These tend to be the politicians, who deal with the most important affairs – the affairs of the state. Without them, politics and nation-building would simply not be possible.

The women descended from the Earth are also highly valued. They include, for example, the great female poet Sappho, who lived on the island of Lesbos (which is where lesbians get their name).

The women who descend from the moon, on the other hand, are the adulteresses and the strumpets. For the men, the same is true – they are the philanderers and the fornicators.

Conclusion

Aristophanes, therefore, turned everything on its head. For him love between a man and a woman is inferior. But whether he meant it seriously? Or is it merely the fancy of a comedian who, above all, wants to make his audience laugh? The idea of a spherical human being is really quite peculiar. I have never seen such a depiction, and I can hardly imagine exactly what a spherical human of this sort would look like.

Beginning of the tour (6.4)

In the meantime, our tour returned to the entrance of Hampton Court Palace, just as the tour was scheduled to begin. A large crowd had already gathered, and Houston recognized Miroslav from a distance. He came over to us and introduced me to him. The very first impression I got of Miroslav confirmed that this man was the very best fit for us. This impression was only enhanced when he began his lecture.

Henry VIII

He did not overload his listeners with details nor overwhelm them with endless series of dates. He presented the human that lived in this palace and only in this way did the walls come alive. In the center of this palace stood Henry VIII. It was his favorite residence. He lived in this magnificent palace, a place he was constantly reconstructing, expanding, and embellishing, with all of his six wives and children. Each of his wives received an elaborately designed apartment. Living spaces were also created for more than 1,000 courtiers and servants. During the French ambassador's visit, an extra 200 guests were accommodated. (The famous painting "The Ambassadors" by Holbein was painted during that visit.)

The kitchens

The young Henry was a giant. He was 1.87 meters tall and had a voracious appetite. The most important thing for him was a table so lavishly loaded that the "boards bowed". Once the king had taken over the castle, the first building works were the expansion of the kitchens to over 50 rooms. Of the many chimneys required for this, 121 still remain today. They are wonderfully decorated in an ornamental style with bricks. The wealth of an owner could be gathered from the chimneys, as they showed that this palace allowed for dining in abundance.

Tudor dishes

The dishes of the Tudor era include the finest pies and sugar cakes. Lemons and oranges were brought from Italy. There were even pineapples from the world newly discovered by Columbus. Expensive spices like pepper from India or ginger from China were used in abundance, as was wine from the European mainland. There were, of course, also large quantities of meat daily, either grilled on a spit or fried in pans. They calculated for one kilogram per man per meal. Pheasants could not be lacking, nor quails. Fish, even dolphins, were transported into the palace by the servants and served on valuable pewter plates.

The Great Hall

The large hall – 32 m long, 12 m wide, 18 m tall – has an imposing hammer beam roof. It is the biggest room in the palace and served as a dining hall. The walls are covered in sumptuous wall hangings from Brussels, which depict the life of Abraham. Every 50 years, they are carefully laundered in a washing system designed especially for this purpose.

The Great House of Easement

After a luxurious meal the overstuffed stomachs also needed some relaxation. Hampton Court Palace was one of the first palaces in Europe to have flushing communal toilets, with 28 seats for boys and men. With the help of lead pipes, the water came from Coombe Hill, 5 km away. At the time, this was a master achievement and this house of easement can still be admired in the palace moat today.

Compare that to Versailles, the palace of the Sun King (Louis XIV) which would not have access to this luxury until more than a hundred years later. There were only chamber pots. These were carried through long corridors by the servants and had to be emptied. And that for 5,000 people.

Henry VIII and his six wives (6.5)

Catherine of Aragon

Miroslav now arrived at the part of his remarks that were closest to his heart: The living people who inhabited the palace and the illustrious guests who came and went. The living quarters of the first wife of Henry VIII formed the start of the tour. While Henry VIII is the most well-known English king, relatively little is known of his wives. And yet these women, each in their own right, are extremely interesting. Most notably the first, Catherine of Aragon. A wonderful portrait by Holbein shows this unusually congenial queen. Very feminine with soft, lovely features, modest and reserved in the process, genuine Christian humility, despite her elite position. She is said to have embellished her husband's shirts with embroidery patterns.

Her parents

Her parents were the famous Isabella of Castile and Ferdinand of Aragon (this corresponds to present-day Catalonia, the area surrounding Barcelona). As a result of this marriage, the whole of Spain was united for the first time. Once they conquered the last Moorish kingdom of Granada in the Reconquista, the last Arabs were driven from the peninsula and Christianity was re-established across the country.

They gave Columbus the task of finding a sea route to India via the west. At the time it was not yet a given that the Earth was a sphere. This is how Columbus found not India, but America. This error was never cleared up for him. Until the end of his life he was certain that he had alighted in India. This is why he called the inhabitants Indians. In any case, as a result of this discovery, Spain became a world power, and all the dynasties of Europe rushed to join forces with this new center of power through marriage.

Married at four years old

In order that no other ruling dynasty could take away the bride for his eldest son, the English king Henry VII married his son at just three years old to the youngest daughter of the Spanish royal family, Catherine, who was four years old. Both children remained living with their parents initially. At 16 years old, however, Catherine had to make the journey to England to her husband, Arthur Tudor. He was 15 years old at the time. And the marriage was officially consummated.

Catherine was ideally qualified. She had a command of multiple languages, including Latin, which was still in common usage at the time. Latin was the lingua franca, used not only in the church, but also as a working language in all European universities.

Early death

The 15-year-old heir to the throne died entirely unexpectedly just five months after the wedding. Both Catherine and Arthur were very ill. She survived the illness. He, unfortunately, did not. He had a disease common at the time, tuberculosis, which could not be cured. So, at 16 years old Catherine was already a widow. Consideration was given as to whether it would be best for her to join a convent. Years of uncertainty followed. The second-eldest son of the king, however, decided when he was 18 years old that he wanted to marry this Catherine, with her wealthy Spanish background. She was eight years older than him at 26, but full of charm. It appeared that the young Henry was genuinely in love with the still very pretty young woman. Moreover, when he died on April 21st, 1509, his father had bidden him to marry Catherine, who was extremely popular with the people.

Annulment of the first marriage

According to the interpretation of the Catholic Church at the time, marriage was a one-time event. Catherine could not automatically go ahead with a second marriage. For that reason, her first marriage was annulled: due to the 15-year old's youth, the marriage was allegedly not consummated. Now nothing stood in the way of marriage to Henry VIII.

Fertility

The young Henry was in a hurry. Catherine became pregnant almost immediately. It was fewer than eight months until she gave birth a daughter on January 31st, 1510. Sadly, this child died on the day it was born. The second pregnancy began in the same year and on January 1st, 1511 a son and heir made a happy entrance into the world. Henry, Duke of Cornwall. But this child also died 50 days after his birth. After a stillbirth in 1512, another son was born in November 1513. As he died on the same day he was born, he did not even receive a name. He was anonymous. The next son, Henry, Duke of Cornwall, who came into the world in December 1514, also died after only a few days.

Finally, on February 18th, 1516, she brought a living child into the world, but it was a daughter, Mary, who later came to be known as Bloody Mary.

In England only male offspring could be given royal dignity. The close relative of Henry VIII, the King of Scotland, was already rubbing his hands with glee, because he reckoned that the English crown would now fall to his children.

A further pregnancy became necessary and resulted in the birth of a daughter. Unfortunately, this child also died on the day of her birth, November 10th, 1518. This birth led to such serious complications that it became clear that Catherine could not bring any more children into the world.

This was as much of a catastrophe for her as it was for her husband.

It is suspected that Henry VIII had Rhesus negative factor blood and, therefore, a blood incompatibility existed between the married couple.

Syphilis

Another explanation is that the young Henry had already been infected with syphilis at a young age by a mistress, which he then passed on to all of his wives. This could explain the frequent complications during pregnancy all of his wives would experience. Anne Boleyn also had a stillbirth.

Splendor and misery

Consider that Catherine came from a royal family, which ascended as a world power as a result of the discovery of America. When also considering that she received the most prized princely consort as a husband, Henry VIII, who after the end of the War of the Roses – which his father Henry VII had victoriously ended – had also helped England become a world power, it is astonishing how much suffering she had to endure and how little good fortune was handed to her by fate.

No way out

Yet poor Henry VIII needed a son whatever the cost. He had no other choice but to impregnate all of the ladies-in-waiting. Luckily, they were all pretty women and were not going to refuse the romantic advances of the king. He was, it must be said, an extremely athletic and handsome young man of enormous strength. He had installed tennis courts in his gardens and was an excellent tennis player. And as a soccer player, he counted among the best. Riding was also a given. His greatest hobby, however, was archery.

The number of daughters birthed by his circle of ladies-in-waiting was not counted, but an illegitimate son was also among them. The king was ecstatic.

Henry Fitzroy

The son, born on June 15th, 1519, was also given the name Henry. He also received the royal title Duke of Richmond and Somerset immediately. He was the most senior nobleman in the country. He was going to ascend to the throne. But when he died at the age of 17, this never came to pass.

Intense suffering

All of the affairs with the ladies-in-waiting and the fact that his illegitimate son, Henry Fitzroy, had overtaken her daughter Mary in the line of succession, was a difficult trial for congenial Catherine.

Mary Boleyn

She was the sister of Anne Boleyn and was, like this lady-in-waiting, employed at the king's court. She had two children fathered by Henry VIII. Both of these actually survived: Catherine Carey, mind you she only lived to be 45, and Henry Carey, who arrived in the world in 1526 and died at 70. It is not clear why he did not recognize this second illegitimate son. The likely reason is that he was very enamored with Mary's sister, Anne Boleyn, and hoped for heirs from her. She, nonetheless, resisted his romantic advances, which only served to strengthen the fervor of his love. She agreed only under the condition that he would marry her, though this of course meant he needed to divorce Catherine. The king, astonishingly, respected her wishes.

The most illustrious court in Europe (6.6)

Up until this point, the English court was the most illustrious court in Europe. It even surpassed the court of Medici in Florence. All of Europe's famous personalities went to and from Hampton Court Palace.

Extraordinary man

Henry VIII was not merely an extraordinary sportsman; he was also highly intellectual and artistically talented. He played multiple musical instruments and composed his own musical works and songs which were turned into folk songs. Even to modern ears, the melody of his Greensleeves is mellifluous.

Erasmus of Rotterdam

One of his regular guests was Europe's most famous humanist, Erasmus of Rotterdam. The king could hold discussions on an equal footing with this great scholar. He also recognized the unusual abilities of Thomas More, even making him Lord High Chancellor of England. This is the highest political position in England. He drew up a written defense of the Catholic faith with him, which was in fact largely written by More and for which he received the elite title "Defender of the Faith" by the Pope.

Thomas More

Erasmus considered his friend Thomas More to be the cleverest man in England, a country which in his opinion was particularly richly blessed with intelligent scholars. He dedicated his most successful and widely read work "In Praise of Folly" to his friend.

William Shakespeare

The great English playwright William Shakespeare also lived at this time. He was eagerly supported both by him and later by his daughter, Elizabeth I, and he depicted the life of the King in a royal drama titled "Henry VIII" in great detail and with much appreciation.

The painter Hans Holbein

The painter Hans Holbein, who preserved the whole of courtly life at the royal court in magnificent paintings, was working at the same level as the great painters working for Medici in Florence.

Joanna, Spanish queen of Castile and Aragon

Important visitors were not in short supply either. The elder sister of his wife Catherine, Joanna, came to visit, for example. She was married to the son of the German king, Maximilian. The son of the king had such a striking appearance that he was given the nickname "Handsome", Philippe the Handsome, or El Hermoso in Spanish. She was so in love with her husband and displayed this so openly that it was considered inadmissible for a queen. When she lost her mind following his early death, she went down in history as Joanna the Mad (Juana La Loca).

Charles V

She was the mother of Charles V, who later was chosen to be the German emperor. He also made a first official visit to Henry VIII after his election as emperor and after the Diet of Worms, at which Luther stood before him and recanted absolutely nothing: "Here I stand, I can do no other..."

Marriage politics

Henry VIII wanted to marry his five-year-old daughter Mary off to the 21-year-old German emperor. In this way, the world power of Spain would be allied with the aspiring world power of England. The minimum age for consummation of the marriage was set at 12 years at the time. That would have meant that Charles would have to wait a further 7 years.

This was too long for him and so he married Isabella of Portugal. As a result, the entire Iberian Peninsula was in one hand. He then married his son Phillip II at the age of just two years old to Mary, who he had initially envisaged for himself, who was by then 13 years old.

Big plans

However, these great plans did not come to pass either. As a result of the divorce of Henry VIII from his wife Catherine of Aragon, Mary was disqualified from ascending to the throne. She was therefore no longer of interest as a wife for the Spanish heir to the throne. But when, after the early death of the male heir to the throne, Mary did actually become Queen of England, he married her as a second marriage. He was, however, not the reigning king, but the queen's consort. Unfortunately, there were no offspring in this marriage. Maria only experienced phantom pregnancies. When she died relatively early, Elizabeth assumed power. From then on, Phillip II was England's foremost critic. Particularly when Elizabeth allowed the execution of Maria Stuart, favored by the Catholic side. He built the great Armada, the biggest known fleet in the world at the time. The battle with this fleet was set to decide who would become the future world power. A once-in-a-century storm decided this battle.

Henry VIII as a candidate

It is also interesting to point out that Henry VIII actually put himself forward as a candidate in the German imperial election. He had lower chances than Francis I, the king of France, among the seven electors, however, who had the support of the Pope. The three spiritual electors, the Bishop of Mainz, the Bishop of Cologne, and the Bishop of Brandenburg, were to support the French king, according to the will of the Pope. The latter also had 300 guilders on hand for the purposes of bribery and, as it turned out, just one of the electors was absent from the election. With four votes from seven electors, it was a clear majority. Charles V, who nevertheless had the ability to dish out bribery payments with the help of Fugger's 800,000 guilders, left the spiritual leaders to languish so that they could not afford to follow the instructions of the Pope.

During these remarks regarding the German imperial election, I allowed myself to play the following mind game.

Mind game

What would have happened if Henry VIII had been elected as the German emperor? Of course, he had lower odds than Francis I of France, who was the Pope's favorite and thus also the favorite of the three prince-bishops – and also than Charles V and Carlos I of Spain, who had the richest benefactor in the world at the time (Johann Fugger) on his side, and whose grandfather, the Emperor Maximilian, had urged his German electors even on his deathbed: "Ach nehmet´s ean doch. S´ischt an Bursch a so an fescher." (Elect him anyway. He is such a smart chap – "Fesch" meaning nice, charming, friendly, handsome, strongly built, sophisticated, stylish, ...)

He was only 20 years old at the time. Assume, purely as a mind game, that Henry would have been elected as German emperor in spite of all of this. How different would the course of world politics have been in that instance?

The most difficult and consequential divorce of all time (6.7)

Miroslav declared the divorce from Catherine the most difficult and consequential divorce of all time. Anne Boleyn pushed it through. I will illustrate at what price in the following remarks. Bear in mind how all of these events affected Catherine.

The international political dimension of this divorce

With a divorce on the level among such significant global historical figures, it was not only about the personal. Many factors, often very contradictory, came into play. It initially seemed that it would just be a church-related problem, as Catholic law deemed marriage insoluble and this was also the case here. But of course, canon lawyers will always find a way to circumvent the law. There are many passages in the Bible in which it is the moral duty of a brother to marry the widow of his deceased brother, in order to guarantee her lodgings and income. The passage in which Jesus is asked whose wife the widow will be after the Resurrection, having married seven brothers in succession, is well-known.

Canon lawyers

Luckily, however, the canon lawyers discovered a passage in the Book of Moses which says: "Curse he who sleeps with his brother's wife." As Catherine had been married to Arthur, the brother who died prematurely, as a four-year-old girl, this passage was taken as evidence for a divorce. The divorce was even permitted by the Pope as a result.

Charles V

Charles V, the German emperor and the king of Spain, had something against this divorce, however. After all, he had already married his two-year-old son Phillip II to Mary, the daughter of his aunt Catherine. He was given the opportunity to prevent this divorce by the French king, Francis I.

Francis I

Francis was not happy that he had been defeated by Charles V in the imperial election, and so he wanted to take away his rival's estates in Northern Italy. He invaded with his armies, but he had to accept that the imperial troops retained the upper hand in the Battle of Pavia. He was taken prisoner.

Breach of promise

Charles V behaved gallantly and released Francis I on his honor. But as soon as the freed king had returned to France, he assembled a new army and re-invaded Northern Italy. He did so with the support of the Pope, who did not want to tolerate a neighbor as powerful as Charles V to the north of his clerical state. In the second battle the emperor's troops once more gained the upper hand and Francis I was again taken captive. This time, however, he was held prisoner in Madrid for more than a year.

Financial difficulties

The financial circumstances of the emperor were so catastrophic following the two battles in Pavia that his field commander Frundsberg could no longer pay his soldiers. As he had made the Pope jointly responsible for this second field campaign, Frundsberg made the quick decision to return to Rome with his army to plunder the papal coffers. These coffers were filled with the shrove money that the Pope had collected for the construction of the magnificent St. Peter's Basilica. During this looting, it did not remain. This looting of the entire city of Rome, known as the Sack of Rome, also affected all of the palaces of the wealthy. The Pope himself was captured. He was no longer allowed to approve the divorce of Henry VIII from Catherine.

Pope Clement

It was, incidentally, the Pope who built the biggest church in Christianity and needed vast amounts of money to do so. Clement had the glorious idea of selling the remission of sins for money. Even for the dead. Anyone wanting to shorten the eternal punishments of their mother or father, therefore, could buy what was known as an indulgence.
"As soon as the coins clink into the box,
the soul will fly out of purgatory."
This was what the most successful seller of indulgences, Tetzel, preached. Interesting that this indulgence trade led to the Reformation, with the nailing of Luther's theses to the church door in Wittenberg. The cause for the split of the church was, ironically, the building of St. Peter's.

Pregnancy

Anne Boleyn had by then abandoned her denial of sexual intercourse and was already three months pregnant. Henry VIII, however, did not under any circumstances wish to bring his longed-for son into the world illegitimately. He married Anne in secret, before he was divorced. Since the divorce from Catherine was hopeless, given that Charles V was opposed to it, and the Pope was in his hands, Henry wrote a letter to Luther, enquiring as to how the England church might disengage from Rome, so that he could become the leader of the Church himself, like the Protestant princes in the Empire.

This led to disentanglement from Rome and the founding of the Anglican Church.

Anglican Church

Now the Church of England was independent with Henry VIII at its head. He could push through his divorce using his own power. This would, however, only be recognized by Protestant countries. This divorce had no validity in the Catholic world. But his wife Catherine had to leave her apartment in Hampton Court Palace and live with her daughter Mary in a distant palace.

The great disappointment

Instead of the longed-for successor to the throne, Anne Boleyn brought a daughter into the world. She later became the famous queen, Elizabeth I.

Anne Boleyn (6.8)

The 1000-day queen

This marriage, which had led to the separation of the English church from Rome and to hostility with the Spanish royal family and the Emperor Charles V, lasted fewer than three years. About 1000 days, which lead to Anne Boleyn being given the title "The 1000-Day Queen".

Oath of Supremacy

All English officials had to swear an oath that the separation of the English church from Rome was lawful. Thomas More refused. He remained loyal to his Catholic beliefs. And although he had counted as one of the King's closest confidantes, he was nonetheless sentenced to death by beheading by Henry VIII.

Protect my beard

He took his last walk with poise. He said to the executioner: "Do not cut off my beard. It is innocent."

Incomprehensible

What is incomprehensible, however, is that Henry VIII put the hacked-off head on display on a high pike on London Bridge for days. How is such brutal savagery even possible – that the head of one of Europe's greatest minds and one of the King's best friends could be treated so shamefully?

Drawn

What the king did spare his friend, mind you, was being "drawn" (as in hung, drawn, and quartered) – a last act of grace. A commoner would have been disemboweled before the execution. A cut was made from the throat to the genitals, which would have already been cut off, and then the entire front side of the body was opened and, starting with the pharynx, the heart, lungs, stomach, and guts were ripped out. The delinquent was still not dead. They were supposed to suffer as much pain as possible before they were hacked into a further four pieces for the finale.

Froissart

The great French painter immortalized this procedure in a painting. When you consider that something like this was possible at a time when the cultural renaissance had reached its absolute zenith, you have to ask yourself whether our image of humans is realistic. One would assume that these sorts of cruelties are only possible in archaic societies.

Pardon

Henry VIII also proved vestiges of humanity during the execution of his wife Anne Boleyn. She was to be executed with a sword. This was considered more honorable than the executioner's axe.

Domestic bliss

When Anne Boleyn gave birth to a boy in the second year of marriage, who nonetheless only lived a few days, the happiness of the marriage had already gone so downhill that this event was not recorded in writing even once. For that reason, some historians have questioned whether this birth ever actually occurred.

Third pregnancy

This third pregnancy was not carried to full term. Anne Boleyn was accused of adultery and executed. That she, of all people (the only one of the ladies in the court who had resisted the King's advances and insisted on a marriage – be it for moral reasons or because she desperately wanted to become queen) was said to have yielded to a passionate temptation with a third party, now that she was Queen, it was hard to imagine. These were likely slurs from the party, who were against the divorce and opposed to the separation of the church from Rome.

Vagrants

A dark side of the illustrious Tudor period also needs mentioning. That is the problem of the vagrants.

Cloth manufacturing

The English were already highly innovative. They made many inventions in technology, becoming the pioneers of the Industrial Age. They invented weaving technology which produced the best fabrics in Europe. Velveteen, velvet, and the finest fabrics from the best worsted yarn attracted the highest prices. For this reason, the estate holders of agriculture switched to sheep farming for wool production.

Farm workers

This meant that agricultural laborers no longer had any work, and the small farms were forced to sell their fields so that large, continuous pastures could be created. Once the modest proceeds of these land sales were used up, they were essentially homeless.

Utopia

Thomas More had left his homes to his farm workers and this was so much land that they could cultivate themselves what they needed to live on. But this was the exception. As a general rule, these unpropertied farm workers wandered around the countryside with their families, without a home, trying to scrape a living through odd jobs and also through theft.

In his image of the ideal state, More shows the catastrophic conditions in England as a counter-image to his ideal state, the island nation of Utopia. Karl Marx used this passage from Utopia in his most important work "The Capital" as a means to demonstrate the inhumane nature of the living conditions of the mere wage laborer's in England.

Anti-vagrancy law

Unemployed vagrants were allowed to be whipped. Continuing vagrancy could even be punished with the death penalty. They received a brand mark like cattle so that they could be assigned to their owner. Their children could be taken away from them. To stop them from being able to run away, they could be put in chains and have an iron neck ring placed on them.

Jane Seymour (6.9)

The third marriage of Henry VIII to Jane appeared – after all the turbulence, which had also left its mark on the King – to bring decisive fulfilment. Jane delivered a healthy son into the world. This event on October 12th, 1537 at Hampton Court Palace finally brought the longed-for male heir, after 30 years of reign and three wives. The entire kingdom rejoiced. A poet even wrote: "There is as much rejoicing at the birth of our prince as for the birth of John the Baptist."

Bonfires

Te Deum was sung in all parish churches. Wine and beer were handed out to the populace free of charge and bonfires were lit. In their enthusiasm, guards in the tower fired off 2,000 cannon balls. The church bells, which were to ring until ten at night, were drowned out. The 21-year-old sister Mary – from the first marriage – was the Prince's godmother and 4-year-old Elizabeth from the second marriage carried the oil in the procession which would later be used to anoint him as king.

His mother Jane Seymour, however, did not recover from the difficult, three-day birth and died a few days later. Childbed fever is suspected as the cause. So, the king's greatest joy was accompanied by deepest sorrow, as he had lost his beloved wife as a result of the birth of the heir to the throne.

The fourth marriage

The fate of his three wives, particularly the beheading of Anne Boleyn, did not make the once-coveted king a particularly desirable favorite. Catholic royal families were excluded from the outset. The daughter of the Danish king, who was a possibility, said: "If I had two heads, I'd consider it. As I only have one, I'm not going to take the risk." There was joy, therefore, in finding a god-fearing Lutheran on the Lower

Rhine, a young noblewoman of 24 years, who dared to enter into marriage with "King Bluebeard".

Holbein

He received the commission to paint a picture of this young woman. He boarded the ship, commanded it down the Thames, across the Channel and from Rotterdam up the Rhine to Cleve, where Anne lived. She had been born in Düsseldorf. But she was not prepared for such an elite marriage. She could not command any foreign languages, not even Latin (as was common at the time), and no English whatsoever. When the engaged couple sat opposite each other for the first time, they could only smile coyly. Outside of "no thanks" and "yes please" she not yet been taught a thing. Henry immediately realized that this was not an appropriate queen for him.

Art and reality

Henry was so taken with the beautiful image that Holbein painted of the young Anne that he signed the marriage contract before he had even seen the bride. Now, however, Henry would have preferred not to have consummated the marriage.

Wedding in Greenwich

But simply sending Anne back home would have been an affront against her that she and her family did not deserve. He had to be married, despite everything. To ensure Anne was legally covered, she played a part in this wedding with the planned divorce from the outset. She declared shortly after the wedding that this marriage would never be consummated. This made the divorce quite straightforward. Therefore, Henry paid her off quite generously. She received a settlement so high that the first official act of his son (that is to say, his legal guardian; he was only 8 years old himself) when he became king was to halve her earnings.

As a buoyant Rhinelander, Anne apparently coped with her situation as a divorced queen very well. She was often at the palace and a friend of the sixth wife, Catherine Parr. The king himself described her as "my best friend".

Catherine Howard

Even before the divorce from Anne of Cleves had been finalized, the king had fallen for the 16-year-old teenager Catherine Howard. She was in love with life and had in her young life already had affairs with her music teacher, with her riding teacher, and now with the King as well, who had already taken her into the castle while Anne was still living there.

Court ceremonial

Unfortunately, the exceedingly charming young Catherine did not understand that she could no longer answer every pining devotee now that she was queen. It was not long until she was also convicted of adultery, and the king ordered her beheading.

Gallery

When the executioner wanted to take her from Hampton Court Palace to the tower where she would be executed, she briefly succeeded in escaping and ran into the palace chapel, where the King was praying. She wanted to ask him for mercy. The King did not even interrupt his prayers. Her pursuers caught up with her in the chapel. The gallery of the chapel is considered a corridor of ghosts. It is not just the ghost of Catherine Howard that haunts it, but Sybil, the governess to the Prince, as well. Rumor has it that even the ghost of Anne Boleyn has been sighted there. England is rather abundant in haunted palaces. But only Hampton Court Palace can come up with three ghosts.

I die a Queen

Her last words before the execution were: "I die a Queen. But I would rather have died as a Culpeper." That was her unmarried name.

Catherine Parr

She was the last of the 6 wives and outlived Henry VIII. This woman, an Englishwoman, had a significant pedagogical influence on the young prince, who was six years old at the time of the wedding. She even reunited him with both of his half sisters, Mary and Elizabeth, who had been excluded from the line of succession by the king and declared illegitimate. The young prince learned to read, write, and do arithmetic. His sisters shared some of his lessons. After the death of his father on January 28th, 1547, he became King Edward VI of England and Ireland at just nine years old.

Four marriages

Before marriage with Henry, Catherine Parr had already embarked upon two marriages. Half a year after Henry's death, her third marriage, she secretly embarked upon a fourth marriage. The public was not meant to know that she had remarried just half a year after the death of her spouse. Public decency required this. With her four marriages, she is the queen of England with the most marriages.

Catholic–Protestant tensions

Tensions between Catholics and Protestants took hold in England during the reign of Henry VIII. And this continued after his premature death at 56 years old, when his son Edward VI became king at just eight years old. He had a legal guardian, the brother of his mother who had died in childbirth – Edward Seymour. He was, in the eyes of his Protestant brother Thomas, too tolerant towards the Catholics. He wanted to topple his own brother by way of a plot. When this was uncovered, Edward allowed his own brother to be executed for high treason. However, these events harmed him so severely that there were riots in the country. For most people Edward had become unsuitable as the guardian for the underage king and for that reason John Dudley took over government affairs.

Death at fifteen

An illness, likely tuberculosis, led to an early grave for the young monarch. To avoid the throne passing to Mary, the daughter from the first marriage who was Catholic, Dudley declared his own niece, Lady Jane Grey, as the heir to the throne. In the line of succession, she was the granddaughter of Henry VIII's youngest sister. She was officially declared as the queen and took over the reign for nine days. But the Catholics overthrew her and made Mary, a Catholic, the new queen. Jane's fate as the nine-day queen was sealed with her beheading in the tower.

Bloody Mary

Mary, a Catholic, wanted to make England a Catholic country again. Three hundred executions of Protestants earned her the title Bloody Mary.
Today we know the name Bloody Mary solely as the name of a cocktail.
Her reign lasted just five years. She died at 42. There is much that can be said about her, and much of it positive. She only lived in Hampton Court Palace as a child, however. As Queen, she resided in St. James's Palace.

Phillip II

As the initially estranged Mary had now actually become queen after the divorce of her mother from Henry VIII, Charles V remembered that he had already agreed a contract of marriage for his firstborn son, though 11 years younger, with Mary. This was now realized. Phillip II traveled to England one year after her coronation and the pair were married in Winchester Cathedral.

Phantom pregnancies

Shortly after the marriage, Mary became pregnant. But a child never came into the world. A second, highly dramatic phantom pregnancy followed. Mary remained childless.
So, the only successor to the throne that remained was the daughter from the second marriage, Elizabeth. That signaled simultaneously the final victory for the Anglican church against Rome.

Childlessness

As Elizabeth also remained childless, the English crown was awarded to James I, King of Scotland and son of her greatest adversary Mary Stuart. With this, England and Scotland were unified for the first time.

Charles Stuart

The son of James I married his daughter Elizabeth to Frederick I of the Palatinate, known as the "Winter King". He entered into an alliance with the Protestants in Germany. The Protestant–Catholic antagonism led to the Prague Defenestration in 1617 and to the beginning of the Thirty Years' War. At the same time in England, Cromwell's dictatorship was beginning. He took

Charles Stuart prisoner, and in 1649, a year after the end of the Thirty Years' War, had him executed in front of Banqueting House in London. Cromwell's henchmen wanted to catch him in Hampton Court Palace, but he managed to escape through the garden. He swam along the Thames, but was then captured on an island in the channel. He was executed in front of Banqueting House in London in 1649, one year after the end of the Thirty Years' War.

A bloody era

With this execution, the monarchy in England ended for a time and was succeeded by Cromwell's dictatorship. This was a particularly bloody time for Catholic Ireland in particular. But nowhere near as devastating as the Thirty Years' War that was raging in central Europe at the same time.

End of the tour

With these wide-reaching remarks, Miroslav ended his palace tour.

In the Mercedes (6.10)

After the tour ended, Miroslav drove us back to his house and his wife Mila in his Mercedes. I have seen quite frequently that in England, there are often German cars parked in front of the rich, spacious homes. BMWs, Audis, Volkswagens. This surprised me, since England is, as the country of Rolls Royce and Jaguar, at the forefront of the automobile industry. But Made in Germany still convinces many English people, although this "Manufactured in Germany" slogan was invented as a form of discrimination. The English were not meant to buy any products that came from Germany. But, to the contrary, "Made in Germany" became a brand.

Compliment

I complimented Miroslav on the lively and attractively arranged palace tour. I also explained to him that I would include his stories in my book London Decameron. When he learned that, he said: "If I had known that, then I would have told you about another of Henry VIII's great loves, that is Marguerite de Navarra, to whom he actually made a marriage offer, albeit one she rejected. Marguerite was the sister of the French king Francis I and she also penned a Decameron."

Heptameron

She wanted to write a ten-day history, like Boccaccio. However, unlike those by the Italian, her stories were not invented, but described genuine episodes featuring famous personalities of the time. Unfortunately, she only reached the seventh day. For that reason, it was named Heptameron after the Greek number seven, "hepta". Marguerite de Navarra was an unbelievably intelligent women; she spoke seven languages. And she was also extraordinarily beautiful.

Suitress for the brother

As Francis I had broken his word after the Battle of Pavia, in which he was defeated by Charles V, and after his release by the Emperor had immediately amassed new troops in order to continue the war, he was taken to Madrid by Charles V after the second defeat, where he was kept prisoner for one year. Marguerite traveled there with the aim of asking for mercy for her brother. Charles V, in spite of the breached promise, put mercy before justice once again. Marguerite made such a big impression on Charles V that he also made her an offer of marriage. But he was also rejected. She married a French nobleman with estates in Navarra. His residence was in Pau, in the Pyrenees, not far from Lourdes. She became the mother of the most popular French king, Henry IV.

Henry IV

Dear Miroslav, I have to correct you slightly here. Marguerite was not Henry IV's mother; she was his grandmother. As she was very cosmopolitan, she invited not only the great writer Rabelais, who created immortal figures in Gargantua and Pantagruel, but Calvin, who played a very significant role in Protestantism in France, as well. As a result, her court became a center for this new denomination and her grandson Henry IV became the leader of the Protestants in France. His wedding in Paris was meant to mark a conciliation between Catholicism and the Huguenots.

St. Bartholomew's Day Massacre

This wedding triggered the massacre of several thousand Huguenots. All the Huguenots of distinction had gathered in Paris for the wedding. The murder plot in the night had been negotiated in advance and would also be carried out in the provinces in other regions of France. That this Henry IV would nonetheless go on to become King of France, albeit under the condition that he converted to Catholicism, is a major decision that shielded France from the religious wars that ruined Germany, like the Thirty Years' War.

"Paris is well worth a mass."

This remark is well-known. It implies: In order to gain Paris, one can easily bear listening to a Catholic mass. This is how he justified his breach of faith. Further famous phrases from him: "Le coq au pot" promised every common man a chicken in the pot on Sundays. He was also a famous womanizer. In French that's known as: "Le vert galant". The smallest park in Paris, in the middle of the Seine, was the only park in Paris not to be closed at night in his honor. Amorous students, who were at that time still not allowed girls in their rooms, met there night after night. If it had rained and the grass behind and under the bushes was damp, four or five couples had to share a bench.

The Edict of Nantes

His Edict of Nantes, which guaranteed religious peace between Protestants and Catholics in France, was very beneficial and was only repealed by Louis XIV. It spared France a Thirty Years' War, which had ruined the Thousand-Year Empire of the German nation.

Marriage politics

Miroslav added one more, almost comical, addendum regarding the marriage politics of the time. It is noteworthy that Henry made an offer of marriage to the sister of the French king yet did not hesitate to invade France in the hope of making conquests while the French king was busy fighting in the Battle of Pavia.

Dauphin

A few years earlier he had already taken steps to marry his daughter Mary to Dauphin, the French heir to the throne. This agreement was still valid when he invaded France with his troops. Of England's estates in France, only Normandy remained – the bridgehead of Calais. From there he hoped to conquer Terenburg, a strategically important location. It sat at the narrowest point of the channel of an important military fortress. It was an important bishop's seat with the largest cathedral in France and had been snatched from the French early on as an enclave for the German emperor. Today the place is called Thérouanne. It was radically destroyed by Charles V so that all that remains of interest today are the archaeological excavations.

The Scottish King

When the Scottish King found out that Henry was tied up in France and his wife Catherine had been left to take over government affairs alone, he in turn seized his opportunity to invade England. Francis I took this as a show of support and the planned marriage with Mary was dissolved in favor of the Scottish Princess Mary Stuart. She was married to Dauphin. It was a marriage that did not last for long, however, and the Scottish King did not have much luck in his military campaign against Catherine either.

Catherine as a "commander"

Catherine succeeded in doing the almost impossible by vanquishing the Scottish King, as a woman, even if she was by no means a homebody at the stove. Henry VIII assigned her sole political authority on his departure. The Scotswoman exploited Henry's absence and invaded England with 60,000 soldiers. In the decisive battle at Flodden Fields, 30,000 of his soldiers fell and the rest were worn down. He also died in this battle. Catherine sent his blood-smeared clothes to his wife in France as proof of the victory.

All of these confusing set-ups allow us to see how different the course of history could have been.

Arrival at Mila's (6.11)

Terraced houses

Miroslav and his wife owned a typical terraced house. More than 20 houses strung together, but each with its own entrance and small front garden, which allows the English to keep the prices low so that almost every young couple can afford a home. The highest percentage of homeowners worldwide.

At Mila's

She had been expecting us. The table was attractively laid. She knew that a German friend would be coming along too. Her grandmother was from Vienna and Mila was proud that she had a fair grasp of the German language. We quickly began conversing. German–Polish relations were, quite naturally, a major topic of conversation.

Polish dishes

Mila wanted to serve typical Polish dishes, which was not difficult as there have been many Polish grocery stores in England since Poland joined the EU. In light of Brexit there is widespread uncertainty about whether the Poles will be able to remain there.

Bigos

She considered making stewed cabbage rolls, but instead decided upon the national dish of bigos. This is a one-pot stew of sauerkraut, cabbage, various types of meat, mushrooms, carrots...

Appetizers

Before that, however, there was also an entrée, a cold cut of Krakowska sausage (*kielbasa*) garnished with particularly piquant Polish gherkins. *Borscht*, a soup made from beetroots, with *pierogis*, semi-circular pastry pockets filled with cottage cheese.

Loan words

Mila was convinced that Poles can make the best gherkin dishes and she knew that the Germans had borrowed the work "Gurke" (gherkin) from the Polish.

Quark

The word quark also comes from the Polish. The many dishes the Polish can make using quark convinced the Germans to replicate it and along with many recipes, they also carried over the word "quark ". Mila knew that too.

Interpreter

In the multi-ethnic mix of Poland, Hungary, and even Turkey a translator with knowledge of the local lingo was needed and who then called first Hungary, then Poland, and lastly the German interpreter.

Kretschmer

This is the Polish word for an innkeeper. The Germans did not carry over this term, but this word is still included in many German family names.

Table manners

During the meal, nobody at the table is supposed to speak. But Mila chatted so inspiringly that the meal was not only very good, but also highly entertaining.

Dessert

After dessert, Mila turned the conversation to her hometown of Krakow, a place she loved very much. She considered it the most beautiful of all Polish cities.

Good fortune

It was the only Polish city that was not destroyed during the Second World War. After the fall of Danzig, it was handed over to the Germans willingly, without a shot being fired. When the Red Army approached towards the end of the war, the governor-general Franks evacuated the German troops from the city, which meant that this unique, historic city was not ruined by combat operations.

The year 999

For Mila the year 999 CE is a fixed reference point in history. This year is the first time "Polanen" are mentioned, and that they settled in this region on the Vistula.

Background

Legend has it that long ago the tribal chief Krakus founded a city on Wawel Hill on a dragon's lair, after he had killed the resident dragon. He is the Polish Siegfried, as it were.

Casimir I

Krakow even became capital city under his rule, after Gniezno was destroyed by the Czechs. It was only in the 16th century that Warsaw became the capital. Krakow achieved its heyday under Casimir the Great. During that time, a large number of Germans arrived in the city, as did many Jews. Krakow joined the Hanseatic League and adopted the Magdeburg rights.

Landshut Princes – wedding

Strong family ties to German dynasties led to multiple marriages between Habsburg and Wittelsbach. Elizabeth of Habsburg, the wife of Casimir IV, was even named as the mother of the Jagiellonians. The Bavarian duke, George the Rich, invited her daughter Hedwig Jagiellonica (Jadwiga) to Bavaria as his bride. Today this Landshut wedding is still celebrated every two years.

Veit Stoss

Nuremberg sculptor Veit Stoss also came to Krakow at this time. He received the commission to design the high altarpiece in St. Mary's Basilica. This altarpiece is so rich and resplendent that even a city like Nuremberg would not have been able to afford it. In Krakow, the artist became a prosperous man. His incomparable abilities as an artist working with wood and stone can also be evidenced in the fact that he was allowed to produce the tomb of Casimir IV.

Jagiellonian – University

Copernicus studied at this Krakow university with many German-speaking scholars. After Charles University in Prague, this university is the oldest in Central Europe. He studied mathematics and astronomy. He was actually born in 1473 in Torún, the oldest Prussian city that was founded by the Teutonic order in 1231.

Fruitful collaboration

There are many other famous German names of printers, bell makers, and painters who contributed to Krakow's cultural renaissance. The coexistence of Poles and Germans was therefore very fruitful for both sides.

Chopin

On this topic, remember that Chopin nurtured a lifelong friendship with Józef Elsner, his music teacher. He introduced the young Frédéric to the art of composition and brought him closer to the well-tempered piano of Bach and the musical richness of Mozart. This friendship continued to be nurtured when Frédéric lived in Paris.

Shibboleth

Unfortunately, however, very different chauvinistic clashes between the two ethnic groups began to emerge. During an altercation between the German citizens and the Polish duke, the latter banished the Germans from the city and executed many of them. A German was considered someone who said kolo, miele, mlyn with a German accent rather than in the Polish way. There are often miniscule differences in pronunciation only noticed by a native. The residents of Krakow at the time all spoke German, Polish, and Yiddish. Even the children there grew up trilingual because each population group made up roughly one third. The German children, however, said the "L" like their mothers, while Polish children said velar like their mothers. In writing the Poles wrote a dash through the "L".

S and SS

During Mila's explanation it occurred to me that the Germans south of Cologne and Berlin speak the starting-S of a word clearly. This is the result of close integration with the Romans. The Italians and the French also say the S at the beginning of a word in the same way. North of this line, however, the sonant, Teutonic starting-S has been preserved. You can immediately detect whether someone was born to the north or to the south of this line from the pronunciation of sun, Sonne, soleil, sole. Today this has largely blurred.

Low German and High German

This Cologne–Berlin line actually makes the German language area bilingual. The northern part, in the lowlands, speaks Low German, known as "platt". The High German sound shift did not take place here. This occurred thanks to the close proximity of the Germans to the Romans. Grimm identified the rules of this shift. This is why, in England, they speak of Grimm's Law.

Written language

As a result of Luther's translation of the Bible into Upper German, the administrative language of Saxony, a similar form of which was also spoken by the emperor in Vienna, was replaced by High German as a written language and eventually as a spoken language in the North as well. Today Platt, or Low German, are seen only as dialects.

Sparta and Athens

Linguistic differences in pronunciation have always led to quips and satire. The different pronunciation of the S sound, clear or sonant, made it easy for the Athenians to make fun of their Spartanic rivals. They quoted poetic passages in the Spartan dialect. So, this:

Mondbeglänzte Meeres-Auen
[Moonlit sea meadows]
Became: *Mondbeglänzte Meeres-Sauen*
[Moonlit sea sows]

Distinctive characteristics

Linguistic idiosyncrasies are often a distinguishing characteristic. A German spy who has mastered the French language so perfectly and free from an accent that it cannot be determined whether he is German or French when under interrogation may go on to betray himself as a German as a result of his speech. Unexpectedly, someone involved in the investigation rams a sharp object into his bottom. He cries out "Aua" (Ow!). If he had been French, he would have cried "aie". He knows that, of course. Yet the surprise effect worked so that he reacts reflexively.

Gilead

Incidentally, the word shibboleth originates from the Old Testament (Richter 12: 5–6). It means that the origin of a person can be detected through the smallest differences in pronunciation related to where they come from. (Professor Higgins from the musical My Fair Lady even recognizes the area of London from which a speaker hails.) During a battle for Gilead the evaders had to pronounce the word shibboleth. The pronunciation betrayed whether they were really from the city or its surrounding area. If they were unable to prove themselves as Jews from Gilead with the exact pronunciation, they were slain.

Kirsche and Kirche ('cherry and church')

The difference between these words is very difficult for the French and must first be learned. The breathy "h" does not only cause difficulties for the French. Southern Germans differentiate between ei and ai, *Leib* und *Laib* (body and loaf), something that North Germans cannot differentiate between. They also can't tell the difference between ou and au. Instead of *Blaukraut*, they have to say *Rotkohl* (red cabbage).

Amateur dramatics

After these excursions into the linguistic details of the pronunciation of vowels and consonants, Mila turned the conversation to her favorite topic: dance, theater, and operetta. Even as a young girl she was actively involved in an amateur dramatics group.

The Beggar Student

The clear high point of her "career" as part of this group was her performance of Millöcker's "Der Bettelstudent" (The Beggar Student). The plot of this operetta is set in Krakow and the theme is the praise of the beauty of the Polish woman.

"I made some tender ties."

The tenor sings. He "studied the Parisians,
the most beautiful women in Saxony
in Germany, Hungary, and Vienna."

For the sake of the rhyming scheme, he even praises the beauty of the Creole women.

"But all of this beauty quickly fades away
if you look at the Polish women,
the Polish charm remains unmatched."

Compliment

Mila referenced these lines without false modesty and as a matter of fact, she really was a particularly pretty woman. I had to give her this compliment, quite genuinely.

Augustus the Strong

The mention of beautiful women from Saxony led Mila to mention that Augustus the Strong, the Grand Duke of Saxony, was King of Poland at the same time. In the Green Vault in Dresden you can still see the treasures he accumulated there in his time.

From the hundredth to the thousandth

We went from one topic to another, from the Polish–Lithuanian empire, to which almost the whole of Ukraine belonged, to the Crimea to the heavy topic of Auschwitz. This concentration camp is situated just an hour's drive from Krakow.

Schindler's List

Schindler's factory is also found in Krakow, a place where he managed to protect thousands of Jews from deportation because they were said to be indispensable to the manufacture of products essential to the war effort at his factory.

Michel Friedman

He is famous for his appearance on talk shows on German television. His parents and his grandmother, as a result of Schindler's help, were spared being deported to Auschwitz. After the war they emigrated to France. An inglorious chapter of anti-Semitic riots, which led to the death of six Jews, was the inciting factor for the move. This massacre, which was perpetrated by Poland after Auschwitz was liberated and no Germans remained in Krakow, led to resentment between Israel and Poland which endures to this day. Michel was born in Paris in 1956. He later chose Germany as his place of residence.

Roman Polanski

He also survived in Krakow. He could hide among Polish families, like his father and many relatives. He emigrated from Krakow to England as a result of this massacre after the end of the war, and then moved on to the United States. His film "Dance of the Vampires" is the most well-known.

German-Polish relations

Mila entertained this whole conversation almost entirely alone. Miroslav had probably over-exerted himself on Henry VIII and his wives. So, I asked her how she views the German–Polish relationship. She thought: The past has still not been worked through. A reconciliation is not in sight, there can be no talk of friendship. I could only agree with this, although I regretted this state of affairs as much as she did.

Silesia trip

I was on a trip to Silesia with a group of people who had been displaced from Silesia. Some of them were expelled as children with their mothers, some were the children of refugees.

Homeland

Their emotions ran very high when we arrived in the cities or towns where the buildings of their parents or grandparents still stood. "Look, Uncle Karl's butcher shop is still standing", or "My parents used to run this guesthouse", or "This is the school where we learned to read our first words and to write before we were displaced".

Polish tour leader

She was a pretty, young woman, very friendly, but she was not permitted to say anything about the fact that Germans had once lived here. Even in Wroclaw, with its pretty city center that has been rebuilt in a historically faithful way, she had no idea that Germans had once lived here. She only knew the Polish history and according to this, Wroclaw has always been a purely Polish city. The former Breslau today carries its Polish name, after all.

Jagniątków

For a long period, the house of Gerhart Hauptmann was not allowed to be visited. As the author of the socio-critical drama "The Weavers", he was held in high esteem by the communists and by Stalin, although he later swung towards National Socialism. His house was allowed to remain standing. In the era of the GDR he received a state funeral. His grave is on Hiddensee, where his summer villa can also now be visited as a museum. His home is, however, in Poland. The tour guide could not explain why a renowned German writer and Nobel Prize winner lived in the middle of Poland.

Agreement

Mila had to agree with this assessment. She was also of the opinion that most Poles lacked the sincere will for truth about the German refugees. The relationship between Poles and Ukrainians is similarly dishonest. The conflicts in Lviv, a city that was inhabited primarily by Poles, while the surrounding area was almost exclusively inhabited by Ukrainians, have still not been forgotten today. Areas with mixed populations always create problems if the rights of minorities are not shown consideration.

Galicia

The conflict over Lviv at that time even reached the last Habsburg emperor in Vienna, who wished to find a peaceful solution to the conflict himself. As a result of the outbreak of the First World War in 1914, however, this was foiled.

Königsberg

On the tensions of German and Poles, I must add a parallel in the relationship between Germans and Russians. During a trip to East Prussia, a Russian woman was leading a group. She confessed quite frankly that she had only learned the history of the city as a result of German visitors. She had herself been born in Königsberg, today known as Kaliningrad, but her parents were simply resettled there in 1945 without being consulted.

Königsberg Castle

In order that nothing recalled the history, Königsberg Castle was blown up and a hideously unsuccessful status symbol thrown up in its place, something that everyone would rather be taken down again. However, the demolition costs are too high. The renaming of Königsberg back to its original name – comparable with St. Petersburg instead of Leningrad – is a collective wish. Yet even such a benign correction comes at enormous costs.

Königsberger Klopse

The Russian tour guide had learned the recipe for *Königsberger Klopse* (German meatballs in caper sauce) from the visitors and passed it on to us. With her, we visited the grave of Kant and his memorial at the cathedral that remains intact despite the destruction of the cathedral. As a farewell, she read us a poem by the poet Agnes Miegel about her hometown. Really moving! And what a difference to Poland.

Contemporary witnesses

On this topic, I have to give another example. A close acquaintance came to our city as a refugee with her mother after the war. She hailed from Bydgoszcz, a Polish city with a very high German share of the population. She was still enrolled in school there. German was not allowed to be spoken, certainly not at school. On the route home with her German classmate, however, the pair naturally spoke German together. A Pole who caught up with them with his horse and cart heard the young girls speaking German to each other. He took his whip and struck both eight-year-old girls. This is how the German minority was treated by a Pole, a long time before the war broke out.

Death of father

As a child, the same woman also had to experience her father being beaten to death by Poles in the courtyard of their house, simply because he was a German. These sorts of crimes must also be part of the discussion when it comes to a reconciliation between the peoples.

Katowice

This wealthy industrial area of Upper Silesia voted for Germany in the 1918 vote. However, the Polish government easily captured this area with its army and incorporated it into the Polish national territory. The Germans were not able to fight back as they were not permitted to have an army at that point in time. The coal mined in Upper Silesia is of a higher quality than the coal from the Ruhr region and it can be extracted via open-pit mining. This plunder was approved by the Allies in the aftermath. Nonetheless, such facts should be openly discussed. A fruitful coexistence between states cannot be built on lies, misrepresentation, and the distortion of history.

Farewell

It was already late afternoon when we said goodbye, so animated was our conversation. We headed straight from our hosts to Mari Vanna in a taxi, where the "Panslavics" (a private discussion group of Eastern Europeans) wished to meet this evening. Miroslav and Mila occasionally go along too, but today they had another engagement.

En route in the taxi (6.12)

The route from Hampton Court to Mari Vanna in Knightsbridge in Westminster is relatively long. Particularly given the traffic and jams that belong to the normal daily routine in London. This meant that Houston had enough time to tell me about what awaited us that evening.

Panslavics

The people gathering that evening call themselves Panslavics. This name sounds rather provocative, but is meant in a more humorous way. It implies only that all Slavic people, both those from the West Slavic region from Poland and from the South Slavic region from the Balkans, are welcome. It is a loosely connected discussion group on a completely private basis. You do not have to pay a fee, and regular participation is also not expected. A core group nonetheless meets every month and a discussion topic is usually specified.

Pan-Germanism

Pan-Germanism is a comparable concept. It is, however, more provocative than the concept of Pan-Slavism. This word describes the dream of a Greater Germany, in which all German-speaking peoples would be united, not only Austrians and German-speaking Switzerland, but also the low German dialects, Flemish in Belgium and Dutch in the Netherlands.

St. Paul's Church

The representatives in Frankfurt in 1848 argued over this Greater German solution. Given that the emperor in Vienna did not wish to give up his multiethnic state in in the Danubian Monarchy, a Lesser German solution was decided upon, with the new capital of Berlin, where the Hohenzollern King then resided as second emperor. Though the Habsburg Emperor in Vienna did also speak German, there were many cultural centers and glittering capitals outside of his German-speaking core territories: Budapest for Hungary, Prague for Bohemia, Bratislava for Moravia, Marburg for Slovenia, Ljubljana for Croatia, and so on.

Negative terms

Both terms, Pan-Slavism and Pan-Germanism, are seen as battle cries, calling to mind the criminal goal of unification for the purpose of world domination. However, there are no vestiges of this at our Saturday meeting.

Founding of the circle

This discussion group in Mari Vanna is almost 100 years old. The first who met there were Russian émigrés, who survived by escaping from the Bolsheviks in 1918, first in Paris, and then later moving on to London. They were often penniless, having lost everything in the Revolution. Here in London they often had to live in the cheapest lodgings. Yet they did not want to miss the stately life to which they had been accustomed in St. Petersburg. The Russian Mari Vanna, constructed in the nostalgic style of the Tsars, helped them to remember the glory of earlier times at least a little. They met here for this reason.

Anti-Bolsheviks

After the Second World War, long-standing opponents of Stalinist communism joined them. They were at the time the biggest group in terms of numbers.

Vladimir

He belongs to this group. He works for the government as a simultaneous English–Russian translator. He is the speaker for this evening and gives a presentation on Hitler's attack on Stalin's army in the Second World War. He has access to archives that are not readily accessible to the public.

Yalta Agreement

While Vladimir was born in England, he has a Russian mother. His father was a Russian who fought in the Vlasov army. Following the Yalta Agreement, he was at Stalin's mercy, which would have meant his certain death. He succeeded, however, as one of the few to escape and he was able to go into hiding. His wife also managed to escape to the West.

Vlasov

Admittedly, Houston had to explain to me who Vlasov was. He was Stalin's most successful general. Ilya Ehrenburg even memorialized him in literature. He fought in the area north of Lviv. He defended Kiev, commanded the 20th Army during the Battle of Moscow. He became commander-in-chief during the liberation of surrounded Leningrad (St. Petersburg). He also managed to fight a wedge to the city. His army, however, could no longer be supplied in the achieved positions. Stalin prohibited their retreat so that the soldiers literally famished. The survivors, who were pitifully few, were wiped out by the Germans. Vlasov himself was captured.

Ilya Ehrenburg

I had to ask Houston again. Although I do count myself among the better informed in the Federal Republic, this name was unknown to me. Ilya Ehrenburg was one of the most well-known writers in the Soviet era. He was an enthusiastic supporter of Bolshevism and called on Soviet soldiers to "rape women and girls! Break the pride of the German woman!" Indeed, this happened on millions of occasions. Admittedly this is the case in every war. So, nothing new in that respect. But as Ilya Ehrenburg was a Jew, this request could lead to anti-Semitic sentiments. For this reason, it is not allowed to be quoted. The official comment of the government in Israel was: This quotation was invented by the Nazis and put in Ehrenburg's mouth in order to vilify the Jews.

Changing sides

Back to Vlasov. The traumatic experiences and Stalin's recklessness in sacrificing human lives likely contributed to the fact that he, though he remained a patriot, changed sides and dreamed of liberating Russia from the tyranny of Stalin. For this reason, he named his army the "Russian Liberation Army". In the Prague Manifesto, he set out how he imagined a Russia of the future. He did not want to bring back the Tsardom, but rather hoped to institute a popular democracy.

The Patriotic War

At the beginning of the war, Stalin was still by no means well-established. The majority of the population was against him. But the opposition's weakness lay in the fact that nobody had organized the resistance. It was only the emergency of the attacking external enemy, the Germans, that bound the Russians together. In spite of the crimes of the Bolsheviks and the out-and-out indifference to the monstrous losses on the battlefield, the Russians were brought together by the fight against the external enemy. This is why they speak of the "patriotic war". It was only this war that united a nation riven by class divisions.

Lacking in self-esteem

There are multiple examples for Stalin's knowledge of his own lack of popular backing. His power was based entirely on unparalleled terror. When informed of the attack by the Germans, a surprise to him, he assumed that his generals would seize the opportunity to take him prisoner immediately. He fled from the Kremlin and hid in his dacha. To his surprise, however, the *Politburo* turned up and asked him to take over leading the war.

Aware that even the ordinary soldier was unwilling to fight for communism, he feared that the simple grunts would defect without fighting. For this reason, he ordered the death penalty for anyone who allowed themselves to be captured. Russian prisoners, who after being taken prisoner in Germany were forced to carry out forced labor, and who after 1945 were handed over to Stalin by Churchill, were shot immediately after the handover, although they had been captured three years before.

Parade in Moscow

On the 25th anniversary of the October Revolution, Stalin held a parade in Red Square. At the same time, the Germans were just 40 kilometers from Moscow. The military situation appeared hopeless and the Russian generals should have agreed an armistice long before. Yet Stalin stubbornly remained out of pure self-preservation instincts. The Germans were aiming for his fall from power and that of his party. He would not have escaped with his life. He would have to be held responsible for all of his atrocities before a court. Of that he was well aware. In order that the officers in this parade did not simply shoot at him while marching past, Stalin had decreed that all weapons during the parade should not be loaded with ammunition.

In the Mari Vanna (6.13)

We were the last to arrive. We were stuck in too much traffic. A side room had been reserved. Cynthia and Charles were already there. Lizzy and Douglas were tied up. Everything proceeded very informally. There was food à la carte. Each person could order what they wished. The group was composed of about 30 people. Everyone knew each other very well. The evening began with personal chitchat and good cheer.

à la carte

The names, at least, of the delicious dishes we were served should be listed. The soups alone are enough to make one's mouth water: borscht, solanki, rassolnik, ukha, shchi, okroshka. Indeed, the cold appetizers were also excellent. There are many sorts of stuffed Russian eggs, rich mayonnaise mixed with caviar or herring, or sausage... Pierogi as well. Blini and pelmeni, pirozkhi, matschi, shashlik, beef stroganoff... The Russian lived well in the era of the Tsars.

Prince William

The head of the restaurants is very proud of the fact that Prince William chose to celebrate his 30th birthday at the Russian Mari Vanna, although the British have been embroiled in a hearty feud with the Russians for generations. Hopefully no bugging devices were installed to record the goings-on which could be used to blackmail the future English King.

Dimitri

During the informal first part of the evening I got to know an interesting man in his middle age: Dimitri. He is from Ukraine and his parents ended up in England because they cooperated with Stepan Bandera. To this day, this name provokes controversy. An area in western Ukraine still believes him to be a national hero, others see him as a traitor.

Bandera

I confess that I had not heard of him either. He was a fierce devotee of Ukrainian independence. More precisely, he was not against the Russians, rather only against the Stalinism of the Bolsheviks. Ukraine is the most fertile country; it was the breadbasket of Europe. These productive loess soils are only found in Germany in the *Magdeburger Börde*. The expropriation of the wealthy peasants, the kulaks, in order to turn their fields into kolkhozes, was met with fierce resistance in Ukraine, as is understandable.

Holodomor

As Stalin's Commissars did not manage to break the resistance of the peasants against his nationalization, Stalin ordered the execution of hundreds of thousands of kulaks. The once well-ordered fields could no longer be cultivated. Stalin allowed the stored reserves of grain to be evacuated. In so doing, he created an artificial famine. In the most agriculturally rich nation in Europe, 14 million died of starvation. That was in 1930 and went down in history as the Kulaks tragedy, or Holodomor, which means death by famine. There were even reports of cannibalism.

Nelly

I would like to add a personal experience to this dreadful reality. A Russian-German, who survived this tragedy as a 12-year-old child, reported it to me in the 1980s. She came to our city as a refugee and explained to me how people had cut open the bodies of the recently deceased and cut out their livers and hearts to eat. It was so terrible for her that she confirmed to me that she had shared this memory for the first time with me, and never with anyone else.

Commissars

Stalin's representatives, who murdered the kulaks and allowed the grain to be evacuated, were the so-called Commissars, superior party functionaries. Since the overwhelming majority were Jews, the general masses no longer differentiated between communists and Jews. For the simple folk, they meant the same thing. The hatred for the revolutionaries of the class war or against the Jews was the same.

Collaboration

Given that Hitler was fighting both communism and the Jews, many in Ukraine felt solidarity with him. Following the first German victories in the war in Poland, Bandera traveled to Krakow to offer his services to Hitler. He wanted to fight with him against Stalin. But Bandera and Hitler differed greatly in their objectives.

Hitler wanted to gain territory in fertile Ukraine for the Germans. Bandera could, naturally, not agree to that. The friendly reception of the German troops in Ukraine – the girls wearing flower garlands in their hair and the adults cooperating immediately and without reservations with the Germans – was squandered so frivolously that it could not be converted into a fruitful collaboration.

Bandera was incarcerated, albeit as a privileged guest at the Sachsenhausen concentration camp. He had a two-room apartment with a library, a Persian rug on the floor, and further comforts.

Massacre

At the end of the war, however, Bandera was sentenced to death by Stalin, although he had not been demonstrably involved in the massacres that the Ukrainians had inflicted on the Commissars. All Bandera supporters were executed. He was able to escape under a false name to Germany, where he lived undetected for many years, until the Stalinist secret service tracked him down and shot him in front of his apartment in Munich. Dimitri himself once gave a lecture on these events for an entire evening, taking as a basis the book by Nikolai Tolstoy: "Victims of Yalta".

Nikolai Tolstoy

He is a distant relation of the famous Leo Tolstoy. His research into Operation Keelhaul is set out in his aforementioned book. Solzhenitsyn referred to it in his book "The Gulag Archipelago" and made these dreadful Allied war crimes, for which Churchill and Roosevelt are responsible, known to a broad public.
More than two million Russians living in the West were delivered to Stalin and executed. These included Russians who had already escaped to the West following the First World War. The parents of Nikolai Tolstoy belonged to this category.

The tragedy of the Lienz Cossacks

The first time I heard about this was also through Dimitri, like the massacre at Bleiburg. These events should be known, however, because they continue to have effects on politics today. The resistance of the Crimean Tatars during the annexation by Putin and the conflict between Croats and Serbs in the Kosovo War have their roots in these terrible postwar events.

Crimean Cossacks

Dimitri told me about a friend, a Crimean Cossack, who was not present that evening. His father succeeded in escaping from Lienz in Austria, where the British were assembling the Cossacks to hand them back over to Stalin. Only 500 Cossacks had the good fortune of escaping. They alone survived. The others were all killed. The Crimean Cossacks were on Germany's side and fought against Bolshevism, which for Stalin justified the eradication of this ethnic group.

Cossack cemetery

Today you can still visit the cemetery in Lienz, East Tyrol. It has been restored and was built to commemorate this tragedy. The hundreds of dead who lie buried there fell from the bridge into the Drava River. They preferred suicide to the fate of being handed over to Stalin. "Not exactly our finest hour," is how Attlee, the first Prime Minister after the Second World War, described it. And for him, that settled the matter.

Crimea today

Following the annexation of the Crimea by Putin, there are still concerns today on the side of the Crimean Tatars, who fought for the Germans in the Second World War, and were therefore executed by Stalin. However, the fact is often overlooked that Russia under Putin, who completely rejects Stalinism, represents a completely different situation. Today the West heaps flattery on the Crimean Cossacks because they can be deployed as a weapon against Putin's Crimean annexation. That the same West sent hundreds of thousands to their deaths in 1946 is something that nobody wants to hear about anymore these days.

Presentation by Vladimir (6.14)

We had to end our private conversation. Vladimir's presentation was about to begin. He knew everyone and it was common knowledge that the lecture did not have to be endured from the first sentence to the last; rather, his speech could be interrupted at any time with a question and that such could even turn the discussion in a completely different direction. He began: "As is widely known, Hitler attacked the Soviet Union on June 22nd, 1941 without any advance warning and without a declaration of war". It happened at night, at 3 a.m. Everyone on the Russian side was sleeping. By the time the woken soldiers had pulled on their trousers and realized what was happened, Hitler's tanks had already pushed far beyond the demarcation line."

Advance warning

And yet there had been many advance warning signs. The master spy Dr. Sorge, a German who had access to information at the highest security level in Tokyo, even knew the exact date: June 22nd. But Stalin did not believe him.

Stalin was sure

He was so sure that Hitler would not attack that he had even disregarded Churchill's warnings. After the failed escape and the capture of the Führer's representative, Rudolf Hess, Churchill publicly spread the rumor that Hitler had sought a standstill agreement with England so that he could strike Russia. This was also communicated to Stalin via diplomatic channels.

Stalin is shrewder

Yet Stalin knew that Churchill had for a long time been pushing to cancel the Nonaggression Pact with Germany because he urgently needed help as long as his accomplice Roosevelt was unwilling to enter the war due to the continuing opposition of the American public to a war with Germany.

Question

At this point in Vladimir's remark, Dimitri interjected with a question. He addressed Vladimir by his first name, as is usual in this discussion group, and asked him: "In your view, how was Hitler's attack connected with the flight of his representative, Rudolf Hess?"

Alternatives

He offered the following options:
Hitler wanted peace with England before he attacked Russia in order to avoid a war on two fronts.
He wanted to prevent Stalin from attacking if a second front line was no longer available.
But then Hess's peace mission went wrong. So why did he attack regardless?

Balance of powers

Vladimir had also considered this and had drawn the following conclusions. Stalin had over six million soldiers, 11,000 tanks, and 10,000 planes. At the same point in time, Hitler had three million soldiers, 3,000 tanks, and 1,000 planes. Stalin had positioned his entire army on the demarcation line. He was in a brilliant situation in that he could attack at any time, or not.

Negotiations

When the Hitler–Stalin Pact was agreed, it was clear from the outset that neither side would be permanently committing itself to this treaty. The signing of this treaty was a great surprise as the whole world knew that Hitler was the declared enemy of Stalin, and that Stalin had not given up his aim of international communism: he knew that only when the flag of communism was waving in the most advanced industrialized nation, in Berlin, would the proletariat's global revolution be concluded.

Churchill's midwifery services

Given his experience in the First World War, Hitler had a mortal fear of a war on two fronts. It was the trauma of his life and that of the entire German people as well. He could not envision anything worse than simultaneously fighting against Russia in the east and against France, England, and maybe even the USA in the west. He only dared to wage war against Poland when he was certain that Russia would not attack. The treaty with Russia was the requirement. It was a huge surprise for everyone, albeit not for Churchill. He had convinced Stalin to agree this treaty so that Hitler would fire the first shot in the Second World War. As soon as that happened, Hitler had fallen into the trap. England was still his enemy and Russia could cancel the standstill agreement at any time. But the beginning of war was a certainty, just like the shot of Sarajevo.

Future plans

Immediately after the Hitler–Stalin Pact was agreed, Russia occupied Estonia, Latvia, and Lithuania uncontested. Added to this were parts of Bukovina, which had not been designated in the treaty, and the beginning of the Winter War in Finland. He also occupied the most important oil fields in Azerbaijan. Both

Churchill and Roosevelt had promised Stalin that Roosevelt would deliver armaments to him free of charge. To do this, the ice-free port of Murmansk was required. Finland had to be captured. The occupation of Azerbaijan was supposed to create a link to Iran, where the Americans and the English wanted to supply the Russians with weapons via the Caspian Sea and the Volga. These military conquests prove that Stalin had only signed the pact with Hitler in order to create the best conditions for the war. It is clear that with the signing of this agreement, intensive preparations for the war with Germany began.

Molotov

He was Stalin's most important secretary of state from September 1939 to 1941. After the pact had worked for two years, Stalin's demands grew greater and greater. He was encouraged in this by Churchill. Molotov went to Berlin and demanded that Hitler assent to Stalin's conquests in Bulgaria, Greece, and Turkey. Turkey was neutral and had a well-equipped army of 650,000 men. For Stalin, however, the Bosporus and the Dardanelles were of great significance, because his fleet in the Black Sea was surrounded as long as these straits could block his access to the Mediterranean.

Although Turkey was neutral, it was very friendly to Germany and Hitler did not want to risk this under any circumstances. Especially as it became clearer what the aim of it all boiled down to. It was clear to Hitler that the war was unavoidable. He never responded to Molotov's demands. But the first preparations for the war had to be implemented. The worst-case scenario had occurred: The war on two fronts. In the east and in the west.

Act of desperation

Russia was obviously prepared to attack. The Hess flight was a daring attempt to end the western powers' support of Stalin by depriving Churchill of power. However, as this peace mission failed, conflict with Russia became inevitable. To avoid giving Stalin the advantage of being able to determine the date of the strike, Hitler risked a surprise attack. Hitler confirmed that this attack had kept him awake for many nights and that he had extreme stomach pain. Given that it took this decision, made on June 22nd at three at night to return to a normal life, shows that this decision was far from voluntary.

Public opinion

The start of the war with Russia unleashed huge anxiety among the German public. The first major criticism from large parts of the population followed. General opinion was that Hitler had begun this war out of a pure desire for battle. Virtually nobody knew that it was an act of sheer desperation.

Surprise success

The beginning of the attack appeared to prove Hitler right. In the space of a few days, five million of Stalin's six million soldiers had been captured. More than 5,000 of his 11,000 tanks had been destroyed, along with 2,000 planes. The young fellows who had been captured also had no motivation whatsoever to fight for communism. They were, as Stalin had feared, defectors who, from personal experience, saw no reason to fight for such a regime. Their fathers, as landowners, had been killed, their agriculture expropriated.

Propaganda

Photographers were sent to the front to capture footage for the newsreel in German cinemas, tasked with taking pictures that showed the Slavic sub-humans. The difference from the Germanic master race was supposed to be clear for everyone to see. The future owners of the fertile land in the east were supposed to see themselves as more worthy compared with these sub-humans. The photographers sought out a dozen faces from the five million prisoners, with repulsive features, protruding ears and hooked noses corresponding to a negative Jewish physiognomy as per the stereotypes depicted in "Der Stürmer", an inflammatory newspaper.

Himmler

After the capture of Hess, Himmler had become Hitler's most important minister after Goering. He also went to the front and took a picture of the prisoners. Unfortunately, this was not in his area so he could not intervene here. He was thrilled to see the young fellows who, in his opinion, had absolutely nothing to do with Marxist ideology and, in his opinion, were good-natured and capable peasant lads.

Mistake

With five million prisoners, the Germans were overwhelmed. Instead of welcoming these young lads and showing them an alternative to Bolshevism, they were locked up in prison camps and forced labor camps. Given the lack of food for their own population, they received inadequate nutrition. Many died.

"Father of a murderer"

Himmler is seen as the chief culprit of the "Final Solution of the Jewish Question". On the scale of crimes, he comes in just behind Hitler, but ahead of Eichmann and Höss. Erich Fried, a Jewish writer, enjoyed lessons with Himmler's father for a year. This father was the head of a grammar school and taught lessons in the subjects of Ancient Greek and History himself. In Erich Fried's novel "Father of a Murderer", there are many interesting details about this man. The Himmlers came from an established Basel patrician family. But for Fried, only one thing matters: He is the father of Himmler, the mass murderer. Whatever the classical teacher says about Socrates or Greek history; or how he interacts with a rebellious pupil, only one thing matters: "You are the father of this mass murderer."

Call me John (6.15)

At this point in Vladimir's remarks, a person who had not been at this discussion evening for long piped up. He introduced himself with the words "Call me John". Houston, who regularly attends these evenings, already knew him. Later Houston wanted to give me a few personal hints about him. John agreed with Vladimir's remarks. He also believed that it was without question that Hitler did not want a war under any circumstances at this point in time. Neither against the Soviets nor against the English. From the very beginning he had courted the English as allies. He did not even want conflict with Poland. He wanted an agreement and a peaceful solution, whereas the Poles wanted to incorporate the city of Danzig, which was up to 98% German, into their national territory. John's opinion was that Churchill, under orders from the United States, had thwarted a peaceful settlement.

Halifax

He continued. At the time Halifax was the English foreign secretary and after Churchill's resignation, he was suggested as his successor. Everybody considered him the most capable English politician.

I recall that Hitler had placed great hopes for peace talks on this foreign secretary. As John's comments continued, it became clear to me why nothing could come out of this. Halifax rejected the offer of becoming Prime Minister. He did not wish to fight for a peace that the superior USA would have thwarted in any case. He did not want to fight in vain, he'd rather enjoy his life. For this reason, he volunteered as the Ambassador to Washington, where he could pursue his passion for hunting more easily than in England, where he had always ended his work at Parliament on a Friday and gone out hunting. He introduced himself in his new post as Ambassador to Washington, and, under the applause of senators and congressmen, declared what he saw as the greatest achievement of English diplomacy, namely: "We forced Hitler into war."

Lloyd George

John's statement was news to everyone. Nobody knew this and it caused quite a stir. Indeed, John was able to contribute a further surprise. After the rejection by Halifax, Churchill's successor was supposed to be Lloyd George. He had already been Prime Minister once, and that was at the end of the First World War. He was thus held in highest esteem. He also supported peace with Germany. Churchill, however, was able to thwart this plan by spreading the rumor that this politician of great merit, though he was just 70 years old, was suffering from an early, aggressive dementia and could therefore not be in the running.

The *Berghof*

In 1936 Lloyd George had accepted an invitation to the Berghof in the mountains near Berchtesgaden. Hitler had used all of his charm – and many testify that he really did have plenty of it – to make a good impression. He presented Lloyd George with a portrait with the inscription "To the Victors of the First World War". In so doing, he wished to signal to the former leader in a chivalrous manner that Germany recognized the victory of the English in the First World War. Hitler's charm offensive was successful. Lloyd George published a full-page article in "The Times ", the country's biggest daily newspaper, about his visit to Hitler, full of praise for his politics. It even stated: "I met the greatest living German of our time". This was an image far removed from the demonization of Hitler on the other side.

No negotiations as a matter of principle

This position of Churchill and the Americans, that Hitler should fundamentally not be negotiated with, would certainly not have been maintained by Lloyd George under all circumstances. The latest propaganda film to glorify Churchill, "Darkest Hour", expresses it like this: "You cannot negotiate with a predator as long as your head is in his jaws".

No alternative

Eventually it led to Churchill being replaced as Grand Admiral due to his blatant failure surrounding Narvik and the resignation of Chamberlain, who assumed responsibility for entrusting this failure with the most important position as supreme commander-in-chief with dictatorial powers. The people had not appointed him to do so. This appointment was made without choice. For ten years, nobody dared to trust him with a mandate after the debacle as Minister of Finance.

John's background

John's comments were now so exciting that there was a break during which they were animatedly discussed. We were not sitting at a communal table, but rather at separate tables in large or small groups depending on the level of familiarity. What we also wanted to know: Who was this John really? It was known that he was an American but had lived in London for a long time. Houston even knew that he was potentially professionally involved in politics. John knew so many details that one almost had the impression that he had prepared his contribution. This was further confirmed by his remarks after the discussion break.

John's speech (6.16)

John argued that this is why Hitler did not want a warlike confrontation for the time being under any circumstances. His party was very much an ideological party which wanted to convince the people of an alternative to communism. In order to achieve that, however, he first had to be able to prove successes.

Housing developments

The situation of workers following the First World War was extremely precarious even in the countries that had achieved victory. Hourly earnings and working hours were fiercely disputed, strikes were on the agenda. Hitler wanted to ensure that even the family of an ordinary worker would be able to own their own house with a garden where they could grow their own vegetables, fruit, and salads. The plots in rural areas were to measure at least ten acres per house. As a result, even families with several children could be supported sustainably. These developments still exist today and are mostly maintained and inhabited by the descendants of the original buyers.

In the large cities, where space was not quite so readily available, he built large rows of houses. The front faced the street while the back side was kept free for green spaces. The parallel rows were symmetrical so that the green spaces at the back could adjoin, remaining free of cars, offering chances for children to play there and for adults to sit together outdoors beneath the trees. These developments are still happily in use today.

Strength Through Joy

Hitler was also keen to allow the general public the pleasure of traveling abroad. At that time, a trip to Italy was only really the preserve of the wealthy. He built a large ship with sleeping cabins designed to sail in the Mediterranean. This was meant to allow even the average earner the chance to sail past fire-breathing Stromboli at midnight, climb Mount Etna, visit Naples, Rome, and Florence. An unforgettable experience at that time. The ship was to be named Adolf Hitler.

Gustloff

This name was, however, replaced with the name of the Swiss man who wanted to establish a National Socialist party in German-speaking Switzerland, who was murdered by the Jewish student Frankfurter. In the last days of the war, this ship helped to rescue 10,000 wounded, refugees from East Prussia, women, and children to Denmark across the Baltic Sea. It was sunk by a Russian warship. There were hardly any survivors. This makes it the greatest maritime disaster worldwide.

VW

At the time, a car was still a status symbol. It is astonishing that Hitler also hoped to make it possible for ordinary workers to own a car: the Volkswagen (VW). The creation of this factory had two more special features. A car factory normally has to make advance payments. It must buy the individual parts for the cars, and needs to pay the workers. This usually means taking on a loan. The banks demand interest on the debt. As a result, the cost of a car usually amounted to one quarter for materials, one quarter for wages, and one half for interest. The banks do the best business in this instance. However, the innovation under Hitler was that a worker had to put down a monthly payment before they could buy a car. They would only receive the car once it was fully paid for. The second innovation was that when the car had been paid for and delivered, they were now debt-free. They did not have to pay any interest to a bank, which even today often leads to difficulties. It was only the banks that did not make a killing.

Ford

The largest car manufacturer in the USA, Henry Ford, found this arrangement compelling. He made no secret of his admiration for Hitler. He showed ample sympathy for Hitler's rulings in other matters as well. This made him a figure of resentment in many circles in the United States.

Prora

Another large project was planned for the island of Rugen: a holiday complex for families with many children. Paying for hotels was too much for the average earner, especially if they had several children. Therefore, Hitler commissioned a holiday complex where holiday apartments could be rented. A huge complex, five kilometers long and four stories high, nestled against one of the prettiest sandy coves on the island. It had space for 20,000 holidaymakers at once. Projected onto a season, that's almost a million. At the front they were right on the sandy beach and by the sea. The back side bordered a spruce forest. There were also common rooms at defined intervals. Guest did not need to cook either with small restaurants and pubs included. A family with children was supposed to be able to have an excellent rest here, in the fresh air with walks on the beach, ball games, swimming, and sailing.

But the project was shelved with the outbreak of the Second World War. It was only structurally completed.

Construction freeze

A modern investor recently expressed interest in finishing at least a section of this large building project. The interest was also very high. The holiday apartments were to be sold as individual apartments, which would also have been successful. But then the construction had to be stopped. The banks were no longer permitted to grant the final loans for completion. There was fear that some would consider this Hitler project as useful. Officially, this "monstrous" construction is seen as a prime example of the "architecture of evil". This is how the famous architect Libeskind, who created the new plans for the World Trade Tower in New York and built the Jewish Museum in Berlin, describes it.

The Autobahn

It is well-known that Hitler had started to build the German Autobahn (highway) system. This also poses a problem to some contemporaries. Eva Hermann, a popular presenter on German television, put her foot in it regarding this matter. Of course, we all drive on the Autobahn. That is not forbidden. But she said that it is still used in the full knowledge that it was built by Hitler. This was too much. She was forced to leave the studio during the live broadcast. She also lost her job as a presenter. Her complaint against the dismissal was rejected in court. For those occupying a public position, such a statement is unacceptable.

Hitler Youth

At ten years old, a boy was meant to join the Hitler Youth and a girl the League of German Girls (BDM). The program, featuring sports training, bike tours with overnight camping, and campfires, was very well-adapted to the children's interests and proved extremely popular. Today's youth are often bored and fail to use their free time productively. Discos, weapons, and binge drinking are not exactly a desirable alternative.

A model for other countries

All of these projects were not merely meant to provide enrichment for the Germans; they were also meant to set an example for other countries. In almost all countries in Europe, parties that imitated Hitler's innovations were formed:
In Italy, the Fascists, in 1919.
In Germany, the National Socialists, in 1920.
In Romania, the Iron Guard, in 1927.
In Croatia, the Ustasha, in 1929.
In Spain, the Falangists, in 1933.
In Hungary, the Arrow Cross Party, in 1935.
A national socialist party was even founded in Israel.
In the USA, an organization called "Friends of New Germany in Chicago" was formed in 1933.

Termination

Yet all of these projects, which should show the world that a type of politics for the benefit of the people was indeed possible, had to be stopped abruptly when the imposition of war commandeered the full strength of the national economy. Hitler could not prove to the world that national socialism was a better alternative to the communism that suppressed its people, and which invariably led to great economies of scarcity in every country in which the communist planned economy reigned.

Intention of the peace efforts

If Hess wanted to force the peace with the help of English "putschists", then it was certainly not to strike against Russia, but rather to prevent Stalin from marching with his Red Army to Berlin as soon as he could no longer count on the assistance of Britain, and when the promise of the Allies in the West to build a second front in order to relieve his Russian troops had lapsed. With this, John ended his story and Vladimir continued with his lecture.

Vladimir's lecture, continued (6.17)

With these remarks, you, John, have worked in a proposition that I can heartily support: That is, that peace with England was to be forced so that Stalin would not attack. Stalin had used the two-year standstill agreement to acquire arms. And Roosevelt had supplied him with armaments by way of Vladivostok. The 10,000 tanks and 10,000 planes are evidence of this.

After the failure of the Hess mission, Hitler's attack could only have been an act of desperation. The only chance he saw was in attacking with an element of surprise. And he actually succeeded in that.

Initial successes

However, these initial successes, which had not been thought possible, did not lead to the immediate end of the war. And now the infinite expanse of the virtually uninhabited Russian landscape yawned before them. Hitler's soldiers had to cover thousands of kilometers on foot as there were no passable roads for vast stretches. Winter was also beginning. As an invasion of this scale had not been envisaged, nobody had thought about winter equipment for the soldiers. Despite a record cold of minus 40 degrees centigrade, a record that had not been surpassed since Napoleon's Russian campaign, and which caused the most severe frostbite among the infantrymen, the German troops soon stood just outside St. Petersburg, Moscow and Stalingrad. These three large cities were now surrounded. In Stalingrad, part of the city area was even captured. There was, however, no march into St. Petersburg. Nor was this intended. Hitler did not want to destroy this beautiful city with its unparalleled artistic treasures – the Hermitage, St. Isaac's Cathedral – through acts of war. In the event of its capture, he would also have had the problem of feeding the population of this city of millions. For this reason, Hitler believed that Stalin would now begin peace negotiations. But Stalin preferred to let a million people starve to death rather than entering peace negotiations.

Guerillas

Stalin's refusal to enter into peace negotiations threw up a new problem. The 400,000 men, native and local and many Jews among them, retreated in the face of the advancing German troops, hiding in the densely forested area. The Americans supplied these guerillas with weapons and food from the air. These struck at night. They interrupted the supply route to the front. They also murdered soldiers by ambush. In hindsight, it turned out that more of their victims were Russian collaborators than Germans. The losses they inflicted were enormous as the fighting troops on the foremost front line were without ammunition and food.

Hitler's radicalism

Hitler's reaction to this challenge was: All the better, we now know that the guerillas are mostly Jews. Now we do not need to waste time finding out who is carrying out the attacks, we'll simply kill all of the Jews hiding in the forest. This was the beginning of the Holocaust.

Strategy

The Western powers, the USA and England, had not intended the victory of Stalin to be the end goal. Rather, they wanted as many Germans and Russians to kill each other as possible in order to eradicate both powers and to achieve victory on their coattails. Their principle was to support the weakest. Initially, this meant Stalin.

Dr. Sorge

Hitler's hope that Japan would tie up Russian forces in Vladivostok so that the armaments supplies would dry up from there did not come to pass. Japan did not declare war with Russia. Dr. Sorge, Russia's master spy in Tokyo who had access to all of the most classified information at the German embassy, told Stalin that Japan had not entered the war. This allowed the armies there to be transferred to Moscow, which in turn prevented the city from being surrounded by German troops as had occurred in St. Petersburg. If that had happened to the capital city, Stalin would have had to surrender whether he liked it or not.

Stalingrad

This city on the Volga river, where a million Russian soldiers had already fallen and from which the majority of the city's 600,000 inhabitants had not been able to flee and had therefore lost their lives, was now receiving supplies direct from Tehran. The Americans were supplying the Russians with fresh armaments, clothing, and food via Azerbaijan, the Caspian Sea, and the Volga. The starving Germans, long without ammunition, had nothing with which to counter them.

General Paulus

The situation was hopeless. Yet Hitler decided that a German general could not be allowed to surrender as a matter of principle. He promoted General Paulus to the position of highest general with the implication that he should commit suicide. But Paulus was taken prisoner along with hundreds of thousands of soldiers. Of these, however, only six thousand survived. He survived and was sentenced for contempt at the Nuremberg Trials. When he was taken into captivity, he stressed that he should be captured as a civilian as neither he nor his soldiers had any more ammunition. A part of his army continued to fight in the north of the city, with a small amount of ammunition remaining. Yet the fact that a German general had handed himself in had powerful symbolism. It was the first Russian victory. And it was the turning point in the war as a whole.

Military aid

To save Stalingrad, Roosevelt nonetheless deployed 400,000 lorries. The notorious multiple rocket launchers could be installed on these; these would have been rendered useless without a set of wheels. The Germans had nothing left with which to oppose this contingent.

Tactics

The tactics of the Western powers was to get the Russians and Germans to kill as many of each other as possible. In order for the maximum death toll to be realized, the weaker party should be supported so that the battle did not end too quickly. The weaker party, until the Battle of Stalingrad, was absolutely the Russian side.

Joel Brand

The Germans' shortage of material took more and more drastic forms. As iron was no longer available for constructing canons, church bells had to be removed and melted down in order to obtain material for armaments. In desperation, the Germans offered a deal. They wanted to hand over one million Jews to the Allies in exchange for 10,000 lorries: that's 100 Jews per lorry, Jews who would otherwise have been sent to concentration camps. Joel Brand was the broker and he was, as a Jew, completely trustworthy. The negotiation took place in Istanbul, a neutral location. Churchill was the responsible discussion partner. He rejected this deal. The question is, did he believe it too risky to give Hitler so many heavy goods vehicles? Or were the Jews not worth saving, because they were just poor Jews from the East? Rothschild is reported to have said: "No scroungers in Jerusalem".

Shah of Persia

The father of Reza Pahlevi, known to all of us, was an advocate of Hitler. He was proud that his nation belonged to the Aryan family of nations. He replaced the label of Persia with the name generally recognized today, Iran, which means Aryan. He called 500 Germans to his country as specialist experts and wanted the rich oil sources to be developed by the Germans rather than the English oil companies. Long story short: To prevent this, English troops marched into his country and occupied the entire area.

The distraught leader wrote a letter to Roosevelt and deplored the illegal occupation of his country. They advocated the 14 points of Wilson and the rights of the people to self-determination. Defend us against the illegal occupation of our country. Roosevelt's answer is shared in the following section.

Roosevelt's letter to the Shah

Roosevelt subsequently communicated to the Shah that American troops would soon be occupying his country in order to protect them from Hitler's desire to conquer. These would have liked to see not just the Middle East, but also the Far East, invaded. He also had the intention of conquering North and South America. The Americans would protect him, the Shah, so that this could not be carried out. It had been decided long before that Iran should be occupied so that armaments for Russia could be transported to the front by way of the Caspian Sea and via the Volga.

Turkey

Churchill's plan to supply armaments via Turkey failed because Atatürk had optimally trained and equipped a 650-man army. Even Churchill did not dare to pick a fight with this army. Instead he suggested to the Turkish Prime Minister that he should avoid entering into massive pledges against Germany. The answer was negative. Turkey's long-established friendship with Germany, which had endured since the Empire, was stronger.

Roosevelt's original letter

Roosevelt's answer to the Persian Shah's request to help him in the face of British aggression is interesting. Roosevelt was not ashamed to write something that everyone, and especially the Shah, immediately recognized as a lie: "It can be assumed that Germany will continue its conquest campaigns and expand beyond the borders of Europe to Asia, Africa, and even

America, unless it is prevented from doing so by the deployment of military operations. It is equally certain that the countries that want to maintain their independence must come together in a joint effort if they do not want to be overwhelmed one after the other. As has already happened to a large number of the countries in Europe."

"It is certain that movements of conquest by Germany will continue and will extend beyond Europe to Asia, Africa and even to the Americas, unless they are stopped by military force..." (Date: August 25th, 1941)

Further course of the war in the East

The turning point following Stalingrad, where German troops were defeated for the first time, induced a great swell of patriotism. Despite immense losses on the Russian side, the Germans were increasingly being beaten back. Nevertheless, the Allies did not yet start to build up the second front in the West so longed for by Stalin. Only when Stalin had already conquered Romania and Bulgaria and was at the border of Greece did Churchill start to worry that he might have drawn the short straw in the power play for supremacy. He feared that the Russians could succeed in capturing Berlin before the English and the Americans were ready.

Letter to Stalin

He wanted to find out how Stalin judged the chances of this and sanctimoniously inquired: "Should we continue to bomb the German cities? There is the danger that if we begin peace negotiations in Germany there will be no buildings left for us to hold meetings in." Stalin recognized the ulterior motive, the actual intention, immediately. He answered: "Carry on bombing. Unfortunately, it won't happen that quickly. It's going to drag on a damn long time." He now wanted to stop the Western powers from redoubling their efforts to stop him from being the first to seize Berlin.

Flight to Moscow

Churchill, however, wanted to make sure the chances of Allied victory had not completely disappeared despite the conquests of the Russians. He flew to Moscow. Stalin sat across from him. On a small piece of paper, Churchill wrote: "Romania: Division of winnings 90% Russian, 10% English". He wanted at least 10% of the winnings from the oilfield in Romania to go to England, although at this point in time Romania had already been captured entirely by the Russians. Stalin "ticked it off", marking a small line on the piece of paper, at which Churchill crumpled it up. Churchill was very pleased with this cooperation. Stalin, however, thought: Why should I get involved in a discussion? I conquered Romania, why should I give away 10% of my winnings? Treaties are there to be broken. He lightheartedly assigned 10% of the winnings from Bulgaria for Churchill as well. Even when Greece came up, he agreed that England would receive 90% and he would get just 10%. The battle over Greece was yet to come. The eventual victor was not going to depend on the tick he had so willingly made. Moreover, the entire Balkan region were divided 50%–50%. Here, neither of the two adversaries had a foot in the door. Tito had retaken the Balkans without the assistance of either; that is to say that he, along with his guerrillas, had occupied the areas the Germans had retreated from without fighting because defending these positions in the Balkans would have been pointless if the Eastern front had crumbled. In the following years he was neutral, so none of this 50/50 stuff. A wonderful example of international politics.

Churchill was enthused by his great success. "The more I get to know Stalin, the greater my friendship with him." However, this enthusiasm did not last long. He soon realized that only his own naivete trusted in Stalin's cooperation.

All of Vladimir's remarks were so surprising and striking that I was quite out of sorts. But I was even more surprised by the comments interjected by John. It would not be possible to say what John had said in Germany without a wave of outrage. I recalled the television broadcast in which Eva Herman, a popular presenter, had said something not particularly unusual about the Autobahn, which then lead to an outsized scandal in the Federal Republic.

Criticism

This time it was Houston who was criticizing me. In general, it is the other way around. He said: "I think you have embellished something quite a bit there. Thankfully the reader has the opportunity to watch this scene on YouTube." Alright then.

Correction

After his criticism, I wanted to rewatch this scene on YouTube, but I could no longer find it. Asking an acquaintance revealed that the scandal did not arise because Herman mentioned the Autobahn, but rather because she held the opinion (and wrote in her book) that it is important for the development of small children that they have a fixed caregiver for the first three years, ideally their mother. This is the conclusion of modern psychologists. Sending a child to kindergarten at just one year old is not said to support their development. An outcry ensued. The discussion participants decided that she was strongly advocating a Nazi-like position. Eva Herman's answer was: "When a belief is correct, then it is also not incorrect even if Nazis advocate it". That was an explanation worse than her remarks about the Autobahn.
It was only following this statement, according to my friend's information, that she had to leave the live broadcast. I did not

have the time to correct the testimony of my friend. I have to ask the reader to inform themselves about what actually happened.

Conversations after midnight

As we wished to visit Windsor Castle on the following day, we decided that we would both stay the night in my apartment on Bayswater Road as we could then travel to Paddington Station on foot and catch a direct train from there to Windsor.

I once more turned the conversation to John, the American. Houston had made contact with him on his very first visit to Mari Vanna. He was simply a curious person and wanted to learn more about him. John belonged to a group in the US which had supported Trump in the election campaign. The group "Friendship with New Germany" no longer exists, albeit no longer in an organized fashion, but many of its members are still alive. John advocated the ideas of Franz Spanknöbel. This man believed that genetics are crucial to a person's identity. In the language of the time: Blood is more definitive than birthplace. With that, he wanted to state that the many German Americans, although they were born in the United States, still harbor a strong attachment to Germany. At the time he even wanted German to become the official language in some parts of America, such as Pennsylvania.

Criticism of Houston

What Houston was saying was so completely unknown to me that I said to him: "I bet there's not a person in Europe who knows who Franz Spanknöbel is. Probably not even one in the USA. You can only read your stories if you have the internet available." "You're right but there are still people in the United States who advocate the ideas of these people who feel positively towards national socialism. You can find some of them on Trump's election team."

Untermyer or Untermeyer

Spanknöbel fought against Untermyer, who initiated the first boycott of German goods. A large demonstration of thousands of Jewish protestors smashed all of the porcelain in New York's largest department store, Macy's. German porcelain was the most highly prized among wealthy Americans. In another section of the department store the demonstrators found women's pantyhose made in Germany, provoking them into setting fire to this department even though the owners of the department store were Jewish.

Reaction

Germans, fight back. Do not buy from Jews. This was the German reaction a few days later. The protest was limited to two days. In all publications, photos and placards of this are still shown to this day without mentioning the preceding events in New York.

Holy war

Untermyer announced the holy war against Germany in a radio address. In consultation with all of the relevant representatives of Judaism – with Rothschild, Rockefeller, Roosevelt, Churchill – he proclaimed, "Judea declares war on Germany". This was also printed in the Daily Mail, the largest newspaper. Around the world, 14 million Jews declare war on Germany. This was 1933, much to the chagrin of the Jews living in Germany who immediately distanced themselves from this because they saw enormous disadvantages for themselves therein. The essence of the holy war is that the defeated are not only subjects but completely eradicated, including the women and even all the cattle. Because Saul did not obey, and allowed the king of the defeated to live, God withdrew his mercy and appointed David as king and successor. The prophet Samuel justified God's command. That is what it says in 1 Samuel 15:2–9. Saul was condemned because he did not completely fulfil the order to destroy the Amalekites.

Mercy

The only purpose of sparing the enemy could be to make sure that later generations of Israel had a chance to learn the art of war. There must be enough enemies remaining for the next generations to have the chance to kill them. This is what it says in Judges 11:24.

The seventh day
Windsor Castle (7.1)

As the sixth day had been so inordinately long and exhausting, today, on the seventh day, we wanted to have something of a Sunday. Without a special plan and without engagements, we traveled by train from Paddington Station to Windsor Central in the late morning. We wanted to take our time seeing Windsor Castle and Great Park.
Although I had often been to London, albeit only for a few days at a time, I have never managed to visit this famous castle. I had no idea how enormous these castle grounds are. For this reason, I was completely overcome when the entire building complex in its full vastness came into view.

Historic beginnings

The age of this complex was also a surprise to me. William the Conqueror had already constructed a wooden castle on this artificial hill. The clearly visible landmark of the castle, the Round Tower, today stands on this "motte". The medieval fortifications, the upper and lower courtyards, in which the royal apartments have developed over the centuries, are grouped around it.

One thousand years

Windsor Castle is therefore thought to be close to a millennium old, from its beginnings. This makes it the largest continuously inhabited castle in the world. It is constantly being added to. It has been changed, new bits added, sometimes it has been more of a fortress. In peaceful times, it was a majestic residence.

Main entrance

Of course, Henry VIII also left his mark here. He designed the impressive main entrance. The pomegranate coat of arms of his first wife, Catherine of Aragon, is displayed above the archway and the portcullis.

Prison

However, his small son Edward, his only legitimate male heir, did not like it at Windsor at all. "There are neither galleries nor gardens for walking here. It is like a prison," he is reported to have said.

A safe place

Once his half-sister Elizabeth became queen, however, it was the safest place. She felt protected from her Catholic opponents here, who were constantly attempting to get rid of her by assassinating her. She had a gallery built and covered over the north terrace. In so doing, she created something like a sunroom for the first time.

Headquarters for Oliver Cromwell

His parliamentary forces conquered the castle during the English civil war. And Cromwell set up his headquarters here. Since he could not pay the garrison stationed there, the soldiers were allowed to plunder the castle.

Rupert of the Palatinate

Windsor Castle was the emblematic symbol of the English monarchy. Rupert of the Palatinate – who married Elizabeth, the daughter of the English king, Charles I – wanted to come to the rescue of his father-in-law. Just a few days after the fall of the fortress to Cromwell, he stood with his troops in Windsor, but he was unable to recapture the castle.

Charles Stuart

We did in fact have an audio guide, but Houston knew his way around so well that he could chip in with many details. The German Baroque poet, Andreas Gryphius, who was alive in the same period as Charles I, wrote a tragedy about the aforementioned's death in classical style; in a way, the first Greek tragedy written in German adhering to the rules of the three classic unities. The unities of action, time, and place. He called his tragedy "Murdered Majesty". A German Protestant glorifies an English Catholic-friendly monarch as a martyr of faith. Charles, I had supported the Protestant League. The Winter King, his son-in-law, was its leader. In times of war, therefore, all fronts are often blurred.

Secret burial

In England, Protestantism had been generally accepted. Charles, I had been taken prisoner by Cromwell and in 1649, one year after the end of the Thirty Years' War in Germany, he was executed in front of London's Banqueting House. Faithful supporters, however, transported his body to Windsor in total secrecy. Advantaged by the gloomy night, he was buried without ceremony next to the casket of Henry VIII and his third wife, Jane Seymour. Cromwell and his men never noticed this. His grave still exists there today.

Queen Victoria

Victoria and Prince Albert made Windsor their main shared residence. After Albert's death, Victoria retreated to the complete seclusion of this castle. She commissioned the construction of a mausoleum close to Frogmore House, where she and Albert are interred.

Queen Mary

For a long period, the castle remained uninhabited. Only the spouse of George V, Mary of Teck, who became a widow so early, made Windsor her favorite residence again. A tourist attraction is the doll's house created by her.

Abdication of Edward VIII

Edward VIII gave his abdication speech, which was broadcast on the radio, in one of the rooms in Windsor Castle.
Well-kept secret

In the Second World War, the Windsors officially remained in Buckingham Palace. But the young girls Elizabeth and Margaret were bought to Windsor to be on the safe side. During the day, the King and Queen remained in Buckingham Palace, but at night they returned to Windsor. Early in the morning they returned to London for propaganda purposes.

Retreat for Elizabeth II

Shortly after her coronation, Elizabeth II decided to live at Windsor on weekends. Only the Royal Standard (flag) indicates whether she is at Windsor or at Buckingham Palace.

St. George's Chapel

This is the most important burial place of the English kings after Westminster Abbey. As we have already heard, Henry VIII and his wife Jane Seymour are buried here alongside Charles I. George III, George IV, George V and his wife Queen Mary, Georg, and the Queen Mother (the parents of the current queen, Elizabeth), who are also buried here.
This chapel is also the most beautiful gothic church in England, on a par with the Canterbury Cathedral.

Transfer of George, Duke of Kent

The assassination ordered by Churchill lead to the death of King George V's youngest son and eight of his closest confidantes on August 25th, 1942. Naturally, he was not allowed to be buried in St. George's Chapel. After Churchill's death, however, the royal family allowed his body to be transferred here, where it belongs.

Martyrdom

The role of this dead man and his commitment to ending the murderous Second World War will probably only be fully realized once the mystery of the flight of Rudolf Hess is one day uncovered.

Spontaneous idea

In front of this tomb, it suddenly occurred to Houston that we could go to Couscous Darna together. He knew a Tunisian waiter there who could tell us some very interesting things about Hess.

Couscous Darna (7.2)

Mohamad

This waiter is called Mohamad. He was born in Sidi Bou Said. This is close to the Algerian border not far from Bizerte, the last of the remaining French military stations in Tunisia before the country became independent in 1958. Mohamad learned French when he was still in his homeland and initially worked in Marseille. North Africans are not a welcome sight there. Therefore, he moved on to England where he has now lived for many years. Couscous Darna is one of Houston's many preferred hangouts as he, as an eternal bachelor, very rarely cooks. Having known Mohamad for years, he has become a good friend.

Coincidence

Rudolf Hess's last nurse in Spandau was also a Tunisian. He was born in 1942 in the same village that Mohamad's family comes from. His name is Abdallah Melaouhi. After Hess's death, he appeared at several events and even on television programs, including in England. This allowed the pair to re-initiate their long-broken contact.

Merguez

First, though, we wanted to order. Couscous and merguez, the delicious sausages, were a given. The sausages are a staple food not just in Arabic North Africa, but in French cuisine as well. On that afternoon not much was going on in the restaurant and Mohamad was frequently able to sit with us and talk.

End of the colonial era

At first the conversation was not about Hess, but about the conflicts at the end of France's colonial hegemony. Mohamad and Abdallah had lived through this while they were still children. The latter writes extensively about this in his book about Hess's final years. He also writes about how his own father lost his life in the process. He also does not conceal the fact that the French carried out brutal torture.

Title of the book

The book carries the title "I Looked a Murderer in the Eyes". Mohamad confirms that Abdallah does not just suspect that Hess was murdered – he knows it as a witness. He is likely the only living witness who was not involved in the crime. Two heavily muscled "gorillas" in American uniforms that were far too tight carried out the strangling. The American guard, Jordan, greeted Abdallah with the words "The pig (!!) is a goner" when he was finally led to the body.

Champagne reception

The instigators of the murder, the three Western governors, drank champagne with some officers as the body of Hess arrived at the officer's casino, confirming that the English secret service had successfully completed their task.

Reason for the murder

Why was a 93-year-old murdered? Eventually Hess was the only remaining prisoner in this massive building complex and its large associated grounds. Dozens of guards, nursing staff, and representatives for the Four Powers were tasked with making sure nobody could make contact with Hess. The nurses could not be of German citizenship and they were forbidden to speak with him. Guards watched over him the entire time to guarantee the prisoner's total isolation.

Number 7

He was also not allowed to be addressed by name, instead he was addressed as Number 7. In the newspapers he was permitted to read, all articles containing anything political were blacked out. Hess was not supposed to receive any information about what was happening in the world. He could never find out that the occupied zones had been unified into a Federal Republic, that a Konrad Adenauer existed, that Stalin and eventually Churchill too were no longer alive. He was only allowed to learn of sporting events and natural disasters. For many years he was not allowed any contact with his family. When his son Wolf Rüdiger Hess was finally allowed to visit him in his final years, two chaperones were always present to ensure that the conversation only covered food, clothing, and health problems.

Writings

Everything that Hess wrote, sometimes on toilet paper, was thrown away each day. There was obviously huge fear that Hess could make something public, something that the English secret service needed to prevent at all costs. They allegedly also treated him with psychotropic drugs, which were meant to shut down his memory. This surveillance cost millions;

admittedly paid for not by the prison guards, but by the German taxpayer.

Gorbachev

The Four Powers took turns carrying out the surveillance each month until Gorbachev announced that he found it undignified to continue to keep a 93-year-old prisoner under these conditions after so many years. He wanted to release him at Christmas.

"Now they are killing me"

Hess, who wanted nothing more than to return to his family, is said to have spontaneously said to his son: "Now they are killing me". It was always about a secret that was not allowed to be made public. In order to prevent this from happening, the English secret service obviously saw no other option than to murder Hess before the release as after that he would have been able to speak out about the secret without surveillance.

Secret

Was it an obsession of Hess's or was it really information that the British secret service absolutely had to prevent from being released?

Haushofer

A parallel suddenly occurred to me. The father of his young secretary, Professor Haushofer, who arranged all of the preparations for the Hess flight and made contact with the English coup plotters, was supposed to testify in Hess's case in the Nuremberg Trials. Two days before the appointed day, Haushofer and his wife were murdered by the British secret service at their remote estate in the Bavarian Alps.

Feigned suicide

This double murder was disguised as suicide. Haushofer was forced to write that he wished to commit suicide with his wife. Then he was forced to take arsenic, following which both the bodies were carried to a small wooded area, where his wife was also hanged, but then they were disturbed so that Haushofer's body remained lying under the tree with a rope around his neck from which they wanted to hang him.

Mosaic

The facts of this case were also news to my friend Houston. Mohamad was not aware of the details either. But one stone leads to another until the mosaic is complete.

African campaign

Mohamad told us more about the Germans' African campaign, which he had learned about from his parents. There are also interesting details on that topic in Melanouhi's book. Rommel was highly respected by the Arabs. When the Allied Forces managed to break through to Tunisia, the German soldiers who were wounded and could not escape in time disguised themselves in burkas until the Americans had moved on. This allowed the Germans to then break through to the coast and save their lives which, without the help of the locals, they would almost certainly have lost. English and American soldiers were loathed by the Arabs due to their arrogant manner of posing as colonial rulers.

El Alamein

All German prisoners were assembled here. Churchill and Eisenhower had devised a very infamous way of how these prisoners could be killed. Leaving them to starve would take a relatively long time. For this reason, an assembly point was created in the sandy desert, completely devoid of shade. The prisoners had to undress completely. The African sun was to inflict fatal burns on their unprotected skin. For the Arabs, this was particularly shocking as the Qur'an stipulates that a man must cover his nakedness from the navel to the knee. "See how our colonial rulers, having regained their power, treat humans." This is how Arabic journalists protested, making the plans of the Americans and the British known even in the big cities. The outrage among the population was so immense that the victorious powers noticed that they had lost all respect among the population, which led them to abandon this method of exterminating the defeated.

Rush of guests

Meanwhile, the restaurant had filled up with guests. Mohamad had to serve. He advised us, nonetheless, to read the book by his countryman ourselves. It is entirely credible and furnished with plenty of evidence. It was brought out in French and has since been translated into German as well.

Wunsiedel

The parents of Rudolf Hess had a vacation home in this remote and idyllic village. Hess wanted to be buried there. His gravestone carried the epigraph "I dared", as was his wish. The family would have liked to keep this grave as a place of remembrance. After 23 years, however, it had to be abandoned. The relevant authorities feared it become a "place of pilgrimage" for neo-Nazis. The bones had to be exhumed and burned. The ashes were scattered at sea so that nowhere is there a place to commemorate this man. The memory of him was also meant to be eradicated. Orwell calls this "vaporization".

Spandau

The massive brick building, one of the few to survive the bombing of Berlin, was torn down a day after Hess's death and the entire area was built over with an English supermarket. The German government was not asked. They would also have had nothing to say. Germany still had no peace treaty at this time. According to Churchill's will, such a treaty should never exist; Germany should always remain an occupied country. The areas where the occupying forces live are exterritorial. They are not subject to German governing authority in any matters.

Shukran Jazilan

In between, Mohamad had time to bring us the book written by his countryman. We leafed through it. A photo of this friendly Muslim is found on the back of the cover. The mutual trust between the pair began with the Arabic phrase "Shukran Jazilan", which means "Thank you", and which Hess is reported to have said to him after a short massage. Abdallah did not react at first as he was so confused. He thought that he could not have heard correctly. It was not possible that Hess could speak Arabic. Hess noticed his confusion and then said: "Yu jadu fi nahri mä lä Yujedu fi-el bah-rie". This sentence is a sentence in Arabic with multiple philosophical interpretations. Translated, it means: "That which exists in the river of abundance is not found in the sea, and that which exists in the abundance of the seas is not found in the river".
Hess and Abdallah could communicate in Arabic without the guards stopping them from doing so. The Tunisian reassured them when they asked suspiciously what this babbling meant: "You already know that he is not right in the head. I play along to stop him becoming agitated".

Hebrew

The French prison chaplain, Gabel, who had previously looked after Hess and was acquainted with Abdallah, confessed to him that Hess read the Torah with him. Hess was very interested in the history of the Jewish people. He was also able to compare many Hebrew concepts with the Arabic. It is, of course, widely known that salaam (Arabic) and shalom (Hebrew) derive this word for peace from their shared, Semitic language. Eloah (Hebrew) and Allah (Arabic) were the names of their god before it was replaced with Yahweh by Moses. The common ancestor of both people is Ibrahim (Arabic) and Abraham (Hebrew), whose tomb in Hebron has two entrances: one on the right for the Jews and the other on the left for the Muslims.

Alexandria

"How can the fact that Hess could speak Arabic be explained?" I asked. He was born in Alexandria and spent the whole of his childhood and youth in Egypt. Arabic was his second native language. His father was a merchant. At home with his parents, the young boy spoke German, of course. But all of the domestic staff – cooks, gardeners, caretakers, maids – were of course Egyptian. Children learn languages very quickly and easily indeed and so it was not hard for little Rudolf to communicate in his environment and with the children in the neighborhood in Arabic. When his father returned to Germany, Hess was already 16 years old, but he wanted to retain this linguistic knowledge and he therefore also learned written Arabic so that he could also read and write in it.

Relaxation

Our lunchtime break in Couscous Darna had lasted quite a while. Despite the wealth of interesting information, some things were really quite depressing. We decided to relax in the

Oriental style and to visit a Turkish bath, an Ottoman hammam. We wanted a bath like a pasha in the spa. In the bodily pleasures of the mortal world, the Muslim world far surpasses us. Houston had no difficulties in finding the best of its kind in London.

In Zaibatsu (7.3)

After we spent a long time relaxing in Pasha Spa, we fancied a small bite to eat that evening. Houston was well-acquainted with the quickest travel links. The Japanese restaurant he suggested is located down the Thames in Greenwich. The Japanese know how to prepare delicious dishes that go down very easily. I was much looking forward to it, still carrying wonderful memories of Japanese cuisine from a trip to Japan. Houston also knew a Japanese waiter there who could share first-class information about the war in the Pacific. His father had been involved in the conquest of Singapore, but later ended up in an English prison and was transported to England by boat. Following his release, he then chose to remain there voluntarily. Haruto, his eldest son – our waiter and the co-owner of the restaurant – has an English mother. But he had not forgotten his roots on the paternal side. He regularly flies to Tokyo where he tends to the family ties.

Singapore

We learned from him that turning Singapore into an enormous fortress was a status symbol for the English, for Churchill in particular. It was the biggest in the Far East. When the stronghold fell on February 15th, 1941, Churchill called it the "worst disaster and largest capitulation in British history". They had developed this fortress to be extremely imposing and considered it invincible, with 80,000 soldiers – Brits, but also Malaysians and Indians – stationed there. Some sources even spoke of 130,000.

The brilliant generalship of Churchill set up tightly packed canons around the island pointing towards the sea. It would not be possible for a single Japanese ship to break through here. For this reason, the Japanese arrived overland across the single, narrow bridge that connects the island to the mainland, which was defended by a mere 200 soldiers. The canons could not be turned around and so 30,000 Japanese soldiers captured the enormous fortress in the space of just three days. The official record of history says: The British could not withstand the staggering supremacy of the Japanese. (This however refers only to the 200 soldiers who were guarding the bridge. The actual comparison of the share of 130,000 to 30,000 was gently ignored.)

Plague of rats

The fall of Singapore was, in fact, officially hushed up. To prevent any glorification of Japanese acts of war, the rumor was spread that the Japanese had prepared a biological weapon of war in Singapore by breeding rats infected with the plague.

Stirring up fears

Throughout English history, the British press had stirred up the fear that the Japanese desire to conquer could have led to the capture of the British Isles. Therefore, before the Japanese fleet were able to circumnavigate the Strait of Malacca – the southern tip of India –, passing the Cape of Good Hope in Africa and on to the west coast of Spain, Portugal, and France, before then invading British waters, a bulwark had to be built. The first stage in Singapore, opposite the strait, had to be constructed as soon as possible.

Comparison

The threat the Japanese posed to the English was at that time as a real as today's threat to the USA from North Korea. Kim Jong-Un, "the rocket man", has a rocket that, if everything goes to plan, could fly over the Pacific and reach the west coast of the USA. At double the speed of sound, this would take four hours. Enough time, therefore, to counteract with the anti-ballistic missile system. For the American government, the risk is too great given that the North Korean dictator could build further rockets if possible: "Nip it in the bud". The safest course of action would be to start a war immediately.

Purpose of the Singapore stronghold

Haruto's father believed that the purpose of this center of accumulated military power was a base from which they would be able to conquer China. That's how he had explained it to his son, at least. The British had divided up their zone of influence with the USA in such a way that Shanghai and the Yangtze River formed the border between the spheres of influence. The USA was to be allowed to seize the northern area including Peking and Nanjing. The southern section, including Hong Kong and Macau, was to belong to the English.

Proxy war

Initially, Japan played no role in this distribution battle. It was only going to be destroyed in the planned war with China, so that the Chinese forces would be weakened and could therefore be more easily defeated by the two Allied powers. Japan, therefore, was only meant to be incidentally involved in this distribution battle. But in that respect Roosevelt and Churchill were very much mistaken. It was not Chiang Kai-chek with his colony numbering into the billions who occupied vast areas of mainland China, but Japan, with just 100 million inhabitants.

That's at least how the Japanese view the Second World War, so Haruto remarked.

To sum it all up: Roosevelt and Churchill were forced to personally intervene in the war. The result was that Japan was indeed defeated, but capturing China was out of the question. This vast empire was eventually lost by the English and the Americans because Mao Zedong, an ally of Stalin, exiled Chiang Kai-check from the mainland to the small island of Taiwan.

The Sassoons

In so doing, nonetheless, the Great Powers did get "their foot in the door" of wealthy China – with the wealthiest family, the Sassoons. These were Baghdad Jews whom Rothschild had brought to India, and who on his behalf – now widely intermarried and related to the Rothschilds – took over the global opium trade and quickly became the most influential and wealthiest family in China as a result.

Opium

England won two wars against the Chinese emperor, who wished to prevent the Chinese people from being ruined by the forced sale of opium. But England was victorious, and the Chinese Emperor was forced to allow the open sale of opium. With this, the opium trade in China was officially 'legal'. Even so, the Rothschilds did not want to carry it out in their own name because the drug trade was ultimately still seen as indecent. The same is still true today. For this reason, it was carried out 'officially' by the Sassoons and not by the Rothschilds.

Worldwide trade

The Sassoons sold opium worldwide out of Shanghai, preferably to India. The poppy fields were in Burma, in the Golden Triangle, which was also an English colony. Burma was occupied by the Japanese in the Second World War because it was where the English military supply line was located, which sought a connection to China from India, after Singapore and Hong Kong had fallen into the hands of the Japanese on May 6th, 1942, and ships could therefore no longer dock there.

River Kwai

A famous film and a well-known tune, the River Kwai March, depicted what happened that led to the English prisoners being forced to build the bridge from Singapore to Kwai. Haruto's father commanded the English prisoners during their march there.

Billy

At this point I interrupted Haruto because I had got to know an English prisoner from Singapore, Billy, during a trip to Spain. He was also commanded to build this bridge on the River Kwai and was only released from Japanese imprisonment after the end of the war. I asked him if it was really true that the Japanese had treated their prisoners so badly and committed such terrible crimes of war as has been generally described. I asked him quite directly: "Were you beaten?" The answer was surprising to me: "Name me a nation that does not hit its prisoners". In saying this, he cleared the Japanese in my eyes. I had also often wondered if the American portrayal of the Japanese in the war was true to reality. During my trip to Japan, I established myself that no people on Earth is more friendly, accommodating, or sensitive than the Japanese. It is the most civilized community that exists on our planet.

Burma

Even this rich country was lost by the English after the Japanese had to withdraw. The wealthy Sassoons lost their opium fields and soon all of their palaces in central China as well. Today they reside in the Bahamas. They don't have any money worries. There was still a dispute between Roosevelt and Churchill. Roosevelt wanted to recapture Burma under all circumstances. Roosevelt's opinion was that opium would offer better business prospects than largely war-torn Europe. Churchill viewed it as more important to attack the European mainland to prevent Stalin from capturing it all the way to the English Channel, by England's front door. Eventually Roosevelt was convinced of the urgency of crossing the Channel. Contrary to his convictions, D-Day took priority over the Burmese poppy fields.

Course of the war in the Pacific Ocean

The Americans principally waged the war against the civilian population: That is to say, they bombed the Japanese cities where women remained with their children, while the men had to fight against the Chinese and were forced to cross over to the Chinese mainland. The need for raw materials forced the Japanese to seek oil and steel, not present on their island, where deposits of these did exist. The battle zone stretched out almost infinitely from northern China Manchuria all the way to Indonesia and the Philippines.

Atom bombs

On several occasions, the Japanese wanted to agree peace, but this failed due to a demand by the Americans for an unconditional surrender as in Germany. The goal was a Japanese genocide. When the atomic bombs fell, the entire Asian mainland was still occupied by the conquering Japanese

– in Burma, in Indochina, on the Philippines, in Indonesia. After the surrender, in part several weeks later, the Japanese withdrew from the mainland without being defeated. An ultimate victory there would have been meaningless if all of the women and children at home had been killed.

Reversal

To start with, the Americans were still pursuing the policy of eradicating the Japanese people. But when the Chinese allies under Chiang Kai-check were driven out by Mao Zedong, who was allied with Stalin, the Japanese were needed as allies against communism. This was similar to the situation in Germany, where conscription had even been reintroduced and a national armed force (the Bundeswehr) created to obtain auxiliary troops to fight Stalin.

Japanese relationships with Germany

The brotherhood in arms of both peoples, Japan and Germany, is still often a taboo subject, even officially. However, there have always been excellent cultural and economic ties between the two nations. Trips to Japan count among my most wonderful memories and experiences. Japanese cuisine had also found its way to us now. A good plum brandy concluded this peaceful seventh day and we said our goodbyes to wonderfully friendly Haruto.

The eighth day
Hampstead Station (8.1)

We had been invited to Lizzy's. She had read my book and wanted to talk about it with me, and with Houston of course, as almost all the stories start with him. I had just put them on paper. In order to avoid spending a long time finding her house, we arranged to meet in a pub in close proximity to the tube station. Lizzy had suggested "Spaniard's Inn", a very old and traditional pub in the old English style where Keats and Dickens had been regular patrons. From there she first wanted to take us on a tour of the part of the city where she lived, and which she loves so much, and which she wanted to show us before she hosted us as guests at her house. It was just the three of us today, because the conversation was initially going to revolve around the first part of London Decameron.

Tour

Lizzy knew her way around. She was thus able to show us the shortest route to all of the interesting houses of the people who meant a lot to her. There is no area of London that has been home to as many interesting personalities as this one. Almost every house has a "Blue Plaque", a commemorative sign displaying the name of the famous person who lived there. Our walk triggered many remembrances. The clean lines of the home of Keats, the great romantic poet, are reminiscent of his almost classical verses. The great landscape painter Constable also felt at home here in these almost rural-seeming surroundings. Galsworthy, the novelist, also preferred this area to every other part of London. The artistic family of George du Maurier also moved to Hampstead numerous times. The son Gerald and the famous daughter, Daphne du Maurier, grew up there and later sourced their own residences there. Foreign artists, including Anna Pavlova, Dante Gabriel Rosetti, the exiled Sigmund Freund (his house is a museum today), and Charles de Gaulle also took shelter here during the Second World War. D.H. Lawrence, Edgar Wallace, Jan Fleming, H.G. Wells. Actors such as Peter Ustinov, Kate Winslet, Johnny Depp, Elizabeth Taylor, and Richard Burton. Singers including Rod Stewart and Amy Winehouse. Memories can really be indulged here.

George Orwell

For Lizzy, it was very important that she lived close to the house of her favorite author, George Orwell. His dystopian novel "1984" once against achieved the highest sales figures in the USA this year. His frightening visions of the future, which he put to paper in 1948, are proving in our time to be true in surprising and unpredictable ways.

Animal Farm

After initial failures in his writerly pursuits, his political fable was hugely successful. It is a satire of the Stalin regime. I personally remember this story very well, being the first literary work, I read in English. Our English teacher took the risk of reading it with us beginners. Orwell's fable is well-suited to this because he uses very simple sentences and the straightforward nature of the story makes the text easy to understand.

"Homage to Catalonia"

This is the title of one of his earlier works. During the Spanish civil war, Orwell worked as a journalist for the BBC (British Broadcasting Corporation) in Catalonia. Lizzy wanted to talk about this with us first. But before that, we still wanted to discover Hampstead Heath. It is the highest point in the city, almost 134 meters above sea level and 6 meters higher than the high point of the cross on top of St. Paul's Cathedral. From this hill, there is a wonderful panoramic view over the entire metropolis that is London. Heath is related to the old word for "pagan" (heathen). It means that the landscape here has been left in its original form. For this reason, this massive park is something quite special, an ancient landscape, unique in the middle of a cosmopolitan city.

End of the tour

Lizzy had arranged the walk so that we arrived at her house at the end of the tour. It does not belong to her, but she had the chance to rent it for a reasonably acceptable price. The focal point, of course, was the music room with a grand piano by Steinway and Sons.

"Ella, elle l'a" (8.2)

To welcome us, she sat down and sang the big hit of France Gall, a tribute to Ella Fitzgerald, who she had personally accompanied on the piano. It is also one of my favorite hits. A truly atmospheric welcome. Then she asked me why, at the end of the first part of the London Decameron, where she sings "Summertime" by Ella Fitzgerald, I had not mentioned that she ended the evening with this song as an encore. Douglas had improved a brilliant trumpet accompaniment, which took even her by surprise.

The explanation was more than simple. I wanted to close the first part of the book with this song, but because the text was on the last page, it was accidentally left out and when the text was converted into a PDF, it did not appear in print. How annoying. Ella, elle l'a, elle l'a... Ella, this exceptionally gifted singer, she's got it, she's got it... Namely that indefinable charm, this inexplicable charm, Ella's got it. Ella, elle l'a, elle l'a.

As a fictional character

Lizzy had read the first edition of the London short stories. Several months have passed between its publication and the present day. The division into days is more of a composition principle than a chronological sequence. Lizzy had never appeared in a book as a literary figure before. When she saw herself depicted in a literary work for the first time, she admits that quite peculiar feelings bubbled up inside her. In the fifth chapter, which has the Hess flight as its focal point, Douglas introduced his partner to us for the first time.

Reason for the invitation

The actual reason for the invitation from Lizzy, however, was that a discussion about the four freedoms close to the beginning of the tales had caught her attention. The freedom from fear combined with the commitment to creating a world of peace, without weapons, as is set out in the UN Charter. This was the essence of the discussion during our walk in Hyde Park. The result of our conversation was that the exact opposite is true in world politics. Lizzy asked if we thought that Orwell had interpreted this fourth freedom in the same way. He created four ministries according to the four freedoms. Freedom from Fear became the Ministry of Peace. The state Oceania, that is the entire British Empire with Canada, Australia, and all overseas territories and the USA, created this Ministry of Peace with the goal of creating a world without military threat. But this ministry has responsibility for the armed forces, the air force, and the navy. It creates perpetual conflict with Eurasia, that's the European mainland from Lisbon to Vladivostok. And with East Asia, as well, that's China and the Far Eastern countries including Japan. Those responsible force a never-ending war, supposedly to keep the world in balance. As a result, a world of perpetual, never-ending conflict is formed, rather than a world of peace.

Confession

Both Houston and I admitted that we had actually read Orwell's "1984". But we had either skipped over or since forgotten this passage concerning the four ministries. But now, once Lizzy had given us a clue, it became strikingly clear to us how current Orwell's thoughts were and how far-sighted he was even at the time he was writing. The three-part division of the world into the American West with England and the English overseas territories, the possible realization of a European mainland ruled by Russia (at least this is Putin's suspected aim), and the first global power in China and its East Asian sphere of influence. But as Russia and China have seen through this, and have therefore allied themselves with each other, this is becoming more and more difficult for the US today. They must therefore fight Russia and China, which is a tremendous challenge. Otherwise they will not be the only global power.

Decisive sentence

On her side, Lizzy admitted that she was electrified when she read the sentence in our book that goes: "Before Roosevelt could manufacture this universal peace, the Pax Americana 'Never Again', he first had to enter in to the war against Hitler. This meant, paradoxically, the war had to be expanded to become a world war."

Paradox

This paradox – that you first have to start a war before eternal peace can be ushered in – remains true to this day. Kim Jong-un makes atomic bombs and rockets. A destructive strike against him is almost inevitable. Iran apparently also wants to build an atomic bomb. Israel sees no other alternative than to destroy this country. Putin wants to resurrect the old Soviet Empire and, if possible, to bring the entire European continent under his rule. Without military confrontation, the hawks in Washington believe he will not be stopped.

Peace efforts

Peace efforts are underway around the world: In Afghanistan, efforts to establish peace have been underway for 17 years; in

Syria, in Mali. Venezuela will have to be invaded in the near future in order for peaceful conditions to be established there.

Atomic bombs

In Japan, it was only the atomic bombs that brought peace, which is why Churchill saw them as extremely beneficial. "We saved millions of human lives with these bombs." With that, he meant that ongoing fighting would have led to these victims. Therefore, he was also very proud that the bomb dropped on Nagasaki was named "Fat Man" after him.

Peacemaker

He called the biggest known bomb, which he had decided would be dropped on the city of Moscow, "Peacemaker". He urged President Truman to deploy it on a daily basis, before the Russians could build their own atomic bombs. There must, however, have been forces in the USA that could have prevented that. If he had carried out Churchill's request, perhaps American companies would today be safely mining the immeasurable mineral resources and raw materials of this powerful continent.

The big brother (8.3)

The surveillance state and the slogan "Big brother is watching you" are in reality far more radical today given the advances in technology than Orwell could ever have imagined. Every telephone discussion, every email, everything is recorded around the world. Anyone can be located, no matter where they live. Remote-controlled drones can attack anybody deemed "hostile" or a terrorist. Crude mistakes and the mistaken bombing of a school bus of children in Yemen did not even lead to protests.

The all-seeing eye

Every smartphone, laptop, iPhone, and the like has a lens through which Big Brother can observe you at any time.

BBC

Orwell was a correspondent for the BBC. He reported on the Spanish civil war from Catalonia. His colleagues were Ernest Hemingway and André Malraux. He knew from the ground up how news, particularly from warzones, could be manipulated and adapted for the papers and for television. The first freedom that Roosevelt declared was: freedom of speech, which becomes the Ministry of Truth in Orwell. This ministry determines what counts as truth. It is also responsible for the spread of truth and the correction of truth. If later events make a previous truth unacceptable, they must be corrected. Undesirable people must be retouched out of photographs. Those who later play a role are perhaps copied into earlier images. All of the methods we know from the Russian Revolution, with Trotsky initially standing in the front row, but later airbrushed out, and similar tricks.

Freedom of speech

When it comes to this, everybody thinks of the freedom of the press. And this is how the first freedom is mostly interpreted as well. Roosevelt deliberately avoided this wording after consultation with Churchill. Press freedom has nothing to do with individual citizens. It is exclusively a privilege of the elites to whom the press belongs. Under press freedom, they understand that they can write whatever they prefer, entirely without regard for the facts. The unsuspecting citizen, however, thinks that the journalist is allowed to report freely and without censorship on facts and events so that the general public can form a picture of the political situation on the basis of this objective information, in order to draw reasonable conclusions from it. Admittedly, the press would have this freedom. The sticking point, however, is that the press is not at all interested in that. They do not want to inform. They want to do politics. The press is the fifth power, uncontrolled and omnipotent. It is independent of voters and its power is currently unlimited.

The Ministry of Truth

It's not facts or events or issues that decide what "truth" is, rather it is defined by the press and the radio. As they are the only voice, they have a monopoly, as previously only the church with the pastor in the pulpit had. Orwell bundled the central point where all pronouncements converge into the Ministry of Truth. All state-sanctioned lies, distortions, and manipulations emanate from this ministry into the world.

Newspeak

A new language is required for these messages. Since the state-imposed lies are sometimes too directly contradictory to those experienced with their own senses, "doublethink" must be practiced. Orwell outlined it in the following example: If, for important reasons, the state introduces 2+2=3, then areas will still remain where 2+2=4 must apply; for example, in statics, when building bridges, in space travel. The terrific thing about this is that the citizen learns to see no contradictions in this.

Current example

Houston offered up a current example of this. He clapped enthusiastically as Lizzy laid out this theoretical example and laughed appreciatively. "You have led me to a great idea. Doublethink is actually not that absurd and we are all already trained in this direction. Churchill is celebrated as the only one who had the courage to act against Hitler. He claims that without him the Second World War would never have taken place. He liked to call it 'Churchill's War' officially. On the other hand, one makes Hitler alone responsible for the war. He alone picked the fight and is responsible for all consequence. He can therefore even be accused of the bombings by the English and Americans on German cities and the expulsion of the Germans from East Prussia, Pomerania, and Silesia. These are all merely the consequences of his attack on the Westerplatte in Danzig." At fault are not those who ordered the bombing of the cities, or the expulsion of 14 million Germans from eastern areas, but Hitler, who fired the first shot.

Crimethink

Lizzy chimed in again and condemned what Houston had just said. That was "crimethink", a thought crime. A person would not be allowed to say something like that in Orwell's Oceania, let alone think it. The mere entertainment of thoughts other than what the government wanted was considered a crime. In this case, Houston's crime was to disregard doublethink and to see a contradiction in Churchill's claiming the war as merit but to ultimately charge Hitler with the crime.

Irresponsible?

Another example of doublethink is Churchill's assertion that the development of the atomic bomb cost a billion dollars. Given the sum, he was of the opinion that it would be "irresponsible" to not use the weapon. The development of the weapon would be a meaningless waste of taxpayers' money. But if it were used and killed 200,000 women and children as a result, the money would have been used "responsibly".

Moral bombing

It is the same logic as his moral bombing, that is the justified bombing of cities and their inhabitants. That is what he called the first carpet bombing of Mannheim. When it comes to the distortion of concepts, Churchill is undeniably the greatest there ever was, a "shining light" in our dark world.

Intended?

The promise "No more war!" and the specification of the fourth freedom in beautiful words and Article 8 of the UNO Charter grew into the huge machinery of war and arms, not just in Orwell's novel but in the world of today. Was that an accident or was the deception intended from the outset? If the ostensibly positive-sounding goals had actually been aimed for, they would not have had to be arranged in total secrecy and the populations of the world would have had to be involved in the deliberations. It cannot be denied that the peoples of the world were deceived with the four freedoms and the UN charter.

Freedom of the Seas

The first paragraph of the UNA Charter on the Freedom of the Seas already provides evidence of that. Nobody argues with the fact that shipping on the world's oceans should be free, without piracy or demands for customs and transit feeds from any neighbors. The secret supplementary agreement to this paragraph states that all states in the world must allow unrestricted access for English and American ships. These countries themselves did not receive this access in the seas claimed by the British Empire and the USA.

But England and America could not produce this freedom of the seas outside their own territory even once. Today there is once again piracy, which make the passage from the Horn of Africa off Somalia, for example, difficult even for British and American ships. This passage currently has to be protected by the military. Even the Federal Republic has to take part.

The parallel Europe (8.4)

The same deception was planned with regard to the founding of the European Union. When Churchill suggested it in his Zurich speech, it was clear that the purpose of this union was to downgrade the European populations into protectorates. Every nation was supposed to give up their sovereignty, relinquish their cultural identity; absolute egalitarianism was the name of the game. The differences of the Europeans would only continue to exist in their identification number. "We will champion you", this is treated preferentially, protected, even given the same preferential treatment as a crown colony.

Yet it was also clear that England would not belong to this Europe, but would stand apart as a protective power. The most important point in this was that Germany should be diluted so that it could be suppressed. The voice of Malta, with 30,000 inhabitants, would carry the same weight as the voice of Germany, with 80 million. It is almost funny that Churchill made this assurance to Switzerland, of all places, in his Zurich speech. He obviously believed it possible that the Swiss, who are so mindful of their sovereignty, would fall for this offer.

The third freedom

"Lizzy, you have been so intensely focused on Orwell's novels that now you must tell us which ministry leads the third freedom, 'Freedom from want'. Freedom from desire, need, material requirements?" Her answer was: "That's the 'Ministry of Plenty'." Norman Rockwell painted an abundantly laid table to this end, with a happy family of parents, grandparents, children, like how the celebration of Thanksgiving Day with the traditional turkey is generally portrayed. A life in paradise. In Orwell's writing, however, this Ministry of Plenty actually stands for planned shortages. It imposes sanctions and plans famines because the needy and the homeless are easier to oppress than wealthy citizens. In fact, there is certainly enough old-age poverty and unemployment in our rich industrialized nations today. Entire areas fall into degeneration, like the Rust Belt in the United States, the insolvency of entire cities, in Los Angeles alone there are 60,000 homeless people. This is potentially controlled by the highest power; the breakdown of infrastructure could be deliberate. Orwell would see it that way, in any case.

Freedom of worship

In this regard, everyone thinks of religious freedom. Yet this is exactly what is denied. "Freedom to worship", whatever you want, means that the religion and all denominations are denied. The church has dogmas; a Christian cannot believe whatever he fancies. As religion is seen as intolerant, it must be fought. Freedom to worship is more in line with Voltaire's "Egorgez l'infâme", wring its neck, in this case the Catholic Church. This is a principal claim of the Illuminati and the highest order of Freemasons.

Ministry of Love

The new ethics, the new morality, the Ministry of Love, arises from this second freedom. It is the height of bending of all traditional human values. In the reality of Orwell's state, it is in fact the torture chamber of the regime. Every protesting and non-conformist person of this state ends up there so that he or she learns how to behave and to think as this state dictates. Smith, the protagonist of the novel, and his lover have personal experience in this concentration camp. "Orwell describes it so vividly that I do not want to convey any details", says Lizzy.

Return

Houston and I still had dark memories of it. Rats played a role. We vowed to re-read the novel "1984" in the near future, and to read it thoroughly.

Change of scenery (8.5)

The immersion in Orwell's bleak vision of the future had dampened our mood and made us almost sorrowful, primarily because the current reality comes so close to Orwell's intimations. We needed fresh air to take our minds off it. After a few steps outside, we were already feeling better.

Lunchtime

It was also time to eat. There were numerous Israeli restaurants in this neighborhood. Lizzy was a regular guest there and we could reach the next one in a just a few minutes on foot. Lizzy enjoyed eating kosher food. She was Jewish, something we learned on the way to the restaurant.

An Orthodox Jew?

She was not strictly Orthodox. She confessed us to that she quite enjoys eating a ham roll on occasion, and pork too. At home, however, she follows the strict separation of crockery used for meals containing milk and crockery used for meals containing meat. "The calf should not be cooked in the milk of its mother" says the Bible and this phrase has made a deep impression on Lizzy too. So, Jews are not permitted to have cream in a gravy. Fish and meat are also not allowed to be mixed. But we don't do that either, although it is not even an unwritten law.

International cuisine

The Jews, who live scattered across the entire world, have adopted eating habits from all peoples. They have an extraordinarily rich, varied cuisine. They adopted falafel and hummus from the Arabs. In Arabic countries there is a wealth of pulses, lentils, and peas that is almost unimaginable to us and which are very popular there. The large number of Jews who have lived in Vienna for a long time discovered strudel there. There are flatbreads, bagels, pizza... Ideas from Eastern Europe, Poland, and Russia. Our mood lifted at the mere mention of these delicacies and soon we had also reached Lizzy's restaurant.

Full of the joys of life

Jews are also well-acquainted with fast days, but apart from that their religion is established more around the joys of life, and certainly not around ascetism. The food is sumptuous and large quantities of wine go along with it.

Lizzy's mother

While we waited for our food, Lizzy told us about her family. Her mother comes from Prague, a city that was a significant center of Jewish life even in the Middle Ages. She had even had the chance to study then, which was still a privilege for girls at the time. She studied at the University of Marburg where she came to know Hannah Arendt. She became one of her closest confidantes and together they attended lectures by Heidegger.

Separation

When Heidegger joined the Party in 1933 and became Rector at the University of Freiburg, Hannah Arendt separated from him and became increasingly involved in Jewish issues. The relationship with Lizzy's mother remained intact, but their routes of escape separated them. Lizzy's mother left in good time for the south of France with her parents, where her parents owned a summer house. That was even before the war, straight after the German invasion of Prague.

Internment

Hannah Arendt only escaped to France in 1939 once the war had already started. Although there was no hostile action in the West at the beginning, German refugees were interned as members of an enemy nation. "In Germany, I would be in a concentration camp, in friendly France, I am in an internment camp. What an absurd world", she is thought to have said. Later she succeeded in escaping from the internment camp and was able to escape to the USA via Spain.

Sanary

At first Lizzy's mother and her parents experienced no problems in Sanary. They met a large colony of artists there. Thomas Mann and all of his children – Klaus, Erika, and Golo. The famous writer Feuchtwanger, the painter Max Ernst, brothers Stefan and Arnold Zweig, Joseph Roth, the theater director Erwin Piscator, Egon Erwin Kisch... For a short time, even Bertolt Brecht was there, though he then emigrated to the USA by way of Finland, Moscow, and Vladivostok. Lizzy's mother and her parents had particularly close relationships with Franz Werfel, whom they had already known well from their hometown of Prague.

Internment camp

With the outbreak of the war, however, these "holidaymakers" were also considered as hostile foreigners, since they were German. The exile as a holiday was over and they were interned. After the French surrender, the Vichy government cooperated with Nazi Germany and the Jews were threatened with deportation. All succeeded, however, in escaping, some to Spain and Portugal, others via Switzerland. The family of Thomas Mann fled to California. Stefan Zweig succeeded in escaping to South America. Lizzy's parents and the Werfels went to New York. For this reason, the relationship between the two families continued during the war.

Franz Werfel (8.6)

This writer is known for his novel "Embezzled Heaven". Then, there is also the famous adaptation of the miracle at Lourdes, "The Song of Bernadette". The national epic of the Armenians, "The Forty Days of Musa Dagh", which depicts the death march of the Armenians in the First World War from their home to this mountain in northern Syria a thousand kilometers away. His last work, which was only published after his death, was titled "Star of the Unborn". It is a utopian novel which describes the condition of terrestrials in 100,000 years. This novel sparked my interest in utopian novels, says Lizzy.

Comparative literature

Lizzy initially wanted to study comparative literature and linguistics. The theme of her dissertation was going to be a comparison of Werfel's novel "Star of the Unborn" with Aldous Huxley's "Brave New World" and Orwell's "1984". However, she instead chose a career as a singer and pianist.

Astonishing

Some passages from "Star of the Unborn" are highly unusual when you realize that it was put to paper in 1945, cited Lizzy. Werfel writes: For generations, Germans have been trying "to be popular". Unfortunately, they have not succeeded. But after the Second World War, the Germans forged ahead at the forefront of humanity and altruism. If anyone mentions the word "sentimental humanitarianism", they are arrested for 48 hours. They are the creators of a thankless ethics, of a selfless urgency to save the entire world. And Werfel also adds ironically: They are therefore the real sheep in sheep's clothing. Despite this, they are still seen as wolves by everyone. A second interesting prediction: The only religions that will still be in existence in 100,000 years are Judaism and the Catholic Church.
It would be interesting to discuss how he came to this conclusion.

Nuclear war

It is astonishing that Werfel speaks of a final, Third World War which would be carried out using atomic bombs. After that it would be absolutely clear to humanity that waging wars is an absolute impossibility. Apart from a minor incident, which saw young people stealing atomic bombs from museums and causing a catastrophe with them, the peace was actually held. Werfel does not, therefore, fall for the lies of Churchill and Roosevelt, who preach "No more war!" and promise total global disarmament.

Alma Mahler – Gropius – Werfel

Werfel's wife was with him in Sanary. She was considered the most beautiful woman in Vienna. And very talented, too. She could paint and draw like her father, the famous landscape artist Schindler. She also composed music. Some of her songs have been preserved.

Gustav Mahler

After exciting experiences with a famous lover, Alexander von Zemlinski, and a romantic relationship with the painter Gustav Klimt, she decided – at 23 years old, and after a few flings with Oskar Kokoschka – to marry the world-famous (even at that time) composer Gustav Mahler. Relationships with Arthur Schnitzler, Hugo von Hofmannsthal, and Alban Berg were not excluded by this decision.

Gustav Mahler forbade her from composing. It was said to be a man's work. Astonishingly, she obeyed. Her second marriage was with the architect Gropius, who was known throughout Europe. And lastly with the writer Franz Werfel. All three husbands were Jewish, as were almost all of her previous love affairs, and she was a fervent anti-Semite. An interesting combination. Lizzy's mother reported to her daughter that the time with the Werfels in Sanary was never boring.

Capital of German literature

Since so many interesting writers had gathered in Sanary, this city was known as the capital of German literature at the time. At that time, some of the writers were still able to publish their books in Zurich. They often represented fairly similar opinions. An interesting comparison would be between Heinrich Mann's novel "The Loyal Subject" and his brother Thomas Mann's novella "Royal Highness". The comparison between Feuchtwanger's novel "Jew Suess" with the film from Veit Harlan, which to this day is only allowed to be shown with commentary. The disturbing short story that is the short novella by Wilhelm Hauff should also be read on this topic.

The best of all worlds

Utopian novels occupy themselves mostly with visions of nations which have overcome all of the problems of the real world. Huxley solves social problems by engineering citizens in artificial wombs into predetermined classes based on intelligence and labor. The ruling class, these are the Alphas. The upper class, the Betas... The lowest class, the laborer's, are the Epsilons. These are inflicted with brain damage immediately after birth that makes it impossible for them to seek promotion. "How lucky that I am an Epsilon." This is their motto, which is drummed into them. All citizens are happy with their status. Furthermore, a happiness hormone is administered to each person, a drug ("soma") which also leads to a stable harmony throughout the entire state. Without using an intoxicant on the population, the state would purportedly not be able to function.

Classless society

Communism also strived for the ideal state. A classless society where there is no longer any difference in classes and where everyone can live according to their needs. This was also the promise of Marxism. The reality, however, looked very different.

Nationalism

In contrast to this international communism, fascism understood itself as an affirmation of ethnicity: "You are nothing, your people are everything". In this viewpoint, however, the rights of the individual are almost inevitably lost.

Politeia

Even Plato tried to create an ideal state. He considered 3 classes necessary: The producers, those are the farmers, are responsible for ensuring food for the population; second: the auxiliaries, that's the soldiers, who are responsible for the protection of the population in the face of external attacks; third: the guardians, that is the people with sufficient intellect to sensibly rule a state. However, even Plato's state cannot do without deceiving the public.

Scholarly republic

During the Enlightenment, Plato's ideas were taken up. Monarchies were heavily criticized. Too often the kings' greed for power led to disastrous wars. In the French Revolution, and a few years before in the United States' Declaration of Independence, a state without a king, so a type of people's rule, a democracy, was attempted to be set up.

Kingdom of God

The longing for an ideal state is actually as old as time itself. "Thine kingdom come", as it says in the Lord's Prayer. This desire is identical to the oldest Jewish prayer, the Kaddish. The Kingdom of God, in which injustice, disease, and suffering no longer exist, that is a millennia-old desire of the Jews. The anticipation of the Messiah, who will usher in this state, is still expected by the Jews. They do not accept the Messiah of the Christians. He does not meet their expectations.

Jewish intelligence

"Wow!" I was taken aback by Lizzy's enormous knowledge. It was a real torrent of information, leaving any presentation by a professor at a university in the shade. Yet, she was actually neither a historian nor a professor of literature, but an artist. Where did she acquire such a tremendous memory? I asked her directly. She had to laugh. Then she admitted that she had also already wondered about the origin of the enormous differences in intelligence among different people.

Religion of the book

She thought there were several reasons for this. Certainly, distinct factors are written in the genes, in one's DNA. Another factor, however, is the training of certain brain functions. It is like a sport. Without continual training even a natural talent will not reach the top in running, in the high jump, in skiing, tennis, boxing, or riding. The same is true of thinking. It also has to be trained, from a young age really. Among us Jews this has been achieved through the regular reading of scripture, the Bible. A Jew who regularly attends synagogue gradually learns the entire history of the Jews in so doing, from the creation of the world and Adam and Eve, from the Flood to Moses and the departure of the Egyptians, to King David and Solomon. Finally, he also learns about the Babylonian captivity. This also creates the identity of the community, even if the members have to live among foreign peoples. Even a Jew who identifies as an atheist and therefore rejects the existence of Yahweh knows their way around the specifics of the Bible, for example, Sigmund Freud.

The Qur'an

A parallel occurred to me, with the Qur'an. A devout Muslim should learn the entire Qur'an by heart, even in the original language of Old Arabic. This is the Arabic language that was spoken at the time of Mohammad, 1400 years ago. Luckily the Qur'an is not quite as extensive as the Old Testament. It encompasses just 114 surahs. But even so, learning this by heart strengthens the memory enormously. In our modern schools, admittedly, nothing is more frowned upon than memorizing. Thought training, in mathematics for example, is entirely derided as well. Why should one learn the four types of arithmetic, adding, subtracting, multiplying, and dividing? A little calculator will do all of that without exertion. Our intellect is becoming more and more superfluous.

Ancient Hebrew

For that matter it's not just Muslims but Jews too who should be able to read their holy book in the ancient Hebrew language. For a long time, Yiddish was their everyday language, which was created by modern Judaism as an artificial mixed language of ancient Hebrew etymology and modern word creations. Yiddish, which developed from Middle High German, was no longer desirable following the experiences of the Jews in the Nazi period. The Holy Scripture, however, is still read in Hebrew in synagogues today.

Yiddish songs

The question is whether Yiddish has died out completely. It would be a shame as there is a wealth of literature in this language and an abundance of unbelievably beautiful songs, most of which arose in Eastern Europe in *shtetls*. Perhaps at least some of these songs survive even if later nobody will understand the text anymore.

The Messiah

Following my interruption Lizzy continued her explanation. For you Christians it is clear that Jesus is the Messiah, Christ, the Savior, she said. But his thousand-year empire has still never come into being and you have been waiting for his resurrection for two millennia. In vain, again and again.

The Jewish Messiah

And what do you believe, Lizzy? I ventured to ask. I am no Orthodox Jew, I'm more of an atheist, she said. But now the scattered Jews around the world once again have their own state with Jerusalem as their capital, at least as Trump sees it, I am no longer ruling out the arrival of a Jewish Messiah. He will build the third temple and make Jerusalem his capital and from there "rule the entire world with an iron rod. All peoples on Earth will bow before him and bring him gifts." At least this is what is written in the scripture.

Dome of the Rock

"And what about the sacred sites of the Muslims, the Dome of the Rock and Al-Aqsa Mosque?"
"They were either destroyed or rebuilt in a different location, stone by stone." These are the opinions of the leading Zionists. But that will not matter anyway as with the global government of the rising Messiah, there will only be one religion remaining and one temple where He, the Messiah, will set up his seat.

The Anti-Christ

This image of the Jewish Messiah, however, corresponds exactly to the description of the Anti-Christ as seen by the Apostles, I objected. Christ will not rule with an iron rod, but with love.

Mahdi

Now Houston weighed in. These questions about the end of days are confusing, he said. Muslim believe in the second coming of Mahdi. Even the top politicians of the modern age, like Ahmadinejad in Iran, officially proclaim that they are anticipating the imminent second coming of Mahdi. Mahdi will be accompanied, according to the teaching of the prophets, by Jesus and together they will fight the Anti-Christ.

Maitreya

The Buddhists, in turn, believe in the arrival of Maitreya, a reincarnation of the Buddha, who appears on Earth every 13,000 years. It is astonishing how many posts on this topic are posted on the internet and YouTube in our materialistic world, and how many millions are interested in these posts.

Interruption

I had to interrupt Houston again. Who in God's name is Mahdi, and who is Maitreya supposed to be? I need the internet again.

Lizzy's brother

Then Lizzy surprised us with the news that her younger brother would be coming to London in the coming days and we would get to know him. Following her escape to New York, Lizzy's mother had married, the son of a Rabbi no less, whose ancestors had emigrated to the States in the Tsar era due to the pogroms. After the end of the war, therefore, a return to Europe with her parents was no longer a question. In the meantime, her father had become a naturalized American and her mother did not wish to return to her hometown of Prague, as this was occupied by the Soviets and was behind the Iron Curtain. Lizzy was born in New York and two years after her, a brother arrived as well. Both parents have since passed away.

Josef

The brother is called Josef, like the favorite son of Jacob who had sold his brothers to the Egyptians out of jealousy. He is very proud of being a Jew and also very proud of the 4,000-

year history of his people. But in what is an almost exceptional case, he recognizes Jesus as the Messiah. He is therefore one of the few "Messianic Jews". "We have an interesting discussion in store", said Houston.

Banality of evil

We continued to discuss Hannah's Arendt's writing "Eichmann in Jerusalem" and the concept of the "banality of evil". After escaping to New York, Lizzy's mother had re-established contact with Hannah Arendt, who now held a professorship at Yale University.

What does banal mean?

Hannah Arendt made many enemies with this term, particularly among Jews. Under this term she understood that Eichmann, who was responsible for the Final Solution – that is to say, the deaths of millions of Jews – was not personally an anti-Semite at all. He studied Hebraic studies, had an in-depth knowledge of Jewish history, and had a personal interest in Jewish literature. Much to the dismay of the Grand Muftis in Jerusalem, he arranged the departure of 100,000 young Israelis. He carried out the commands to eradicate even against his own feelings, purely because he believes that the extermination was necessary for the preservation of his own people. Moreover, it was a command. For this reason, he also had no remorse. Even in the glass cage in front of the court in Jerusalem, he felt innocent and pleaded "not guilty".

The radical evil

Does radical evil not exist either? Is every person who breaks the laws of god a poor mentally ill person, who needs psychotherapeutic help? The important theologian and psychiatrist Drewermann represents this viewpoint. And in a certain sense, so does Pope Francis, when he washes the feet of criminal prisoners who do not believe in Jesus, just as Jesus washed the feet of his disciples before the Last Supper. The prisoners need mercy and healing, not a punishment.

The Crucifixion

The Crucifixion, on the other hand, is an irrefutable sign that absolute evil exists. When a person who does only good works, heals the sick, drives out demons, and proclaims God's word, is condemned by the high priest for blasphemy, and handed over to the Roman governor Pontius Pilate to be crucified, then it is clear that the god of this world is Satan, the anti-God, who denies the rule of the true God.

At Antonio's (8.7)

The meeting took place in a restaurant called Antonio's. The theme of the evening was the recapture of Italy. It was the continuation of Antonio's narration of Mussolini's wars, his *guerra parallela*. Which he had announced to us during the evening at Cynthia's.

Guests

Houston had also invited John to this evening, surprisingly. Since American soldiers had made up the main contingent during the liberation of Italy from fascism, he suspected that an American would not be out of place where this topic was concerned. Sure enough, this was confirmed when he unexpectedly contributed a story about the recapture of Italy.

Exiled Poland

Miroslav, who had presented the European history of the royal dynasties at the time of Henry VIII in such an interesting way, was also present as was his wife, Mila, who had described the Polish-German relations in her hometown of Krakow so interestingly. Thus, ten narrators of stories with London as their starting point were assembled for the first time, exactly like in the historical original "Decameron" by Boccaccio.

Dining

There was food à la carte. Guiseppe, who we already knew, was serving officially as a waiter and the chef, Federico, was often seen at the table. The red wine drinkers opted for Chianti and Bardolino. Lizzy preferred sweet Marsala. Frascati and Orvieto were the white wines served. Even the sensational Muscat of Alexandria from Sicily was on the wine list.

Enjoyment without regret

Just reading the menu was enough to make the mouth water. It featured ossobuco, saltimbocca, bruschetta, polenta, bresaola, gnocchi, gamberi, zampone, involtini di vitello, gorgonzola, mozzarella, zuppa di pesce.

Table talks

During the meal, there were no long speeches. The very lively conversation focused only on the private. But then Antonio began his story of how Italy had been recaptured by the Allies.

Uncertainties

The Allies considered several possibilities for cracking the "fortress of Europe". Landing on the Atlantic Coast or invading via the Channel were considered too dangerous because of the Atlantic Wall. It seemed easier to invade from the Mediterranean via Greece, Sicily, or Sardinia. Making landfall in Sicily was decided upon as this was the shortest route from

Tunisia across the sea. The crossing of the sea was the most vulnerable part of the invasion as the relatively slow ships could easily be hit and sunk by the much faster planes.

Deceptive maneuver

Of course, it was also important for the enemy to be deceived about the location of the landing so that they could not set up their main fighting force there. For this reason, a body with secret papers on its person was thrown into the sea, which then washed up on shore in southern Italy. The papers implied that the landing would take place on Sardinia. It is likely that Hitler was deceived as a result. That's because, during the landing in Sicily, there was relatively little resistance.

Preparations

The landing on Sicily was prepared in minute detail over a long period by the Americans. The Sicilian mafia had close connections to the American mafia which had developed from the Sicilian branch in New York. Annihilating the mafia in Sicily was considered Mussolini's greatest achievement, something no one else had managed. In other words, he had eliminated all of the leading figures but the deeper structures, the widely branching families, all still remained. They were contacted by infiltrating guerrillas and cooperated willingly with the American soldiers.

Lucky Luciano

He was the most important man and the boss to end all bosses. Even as a young boy he stood out for his shoplifting and the extortion of his classmates. Only one classmate, Meyer Lansky, fought back and proved in a boxing match that he could take on this thug Lucky. The latter was so impressed that he picked him to be his partner. Since Meyer Lansky was a Jew, the New

York mafia was called "Kosher Nostra" in reference to "Cosa Nostra".

John's contribution

At this point John interjected. He explained Lucky's story. At 14 years old, he wins 244 dollars, hence the name Lucky. After dropping out of school, he spent a period at a school for truants. In 1915, he was thrown out of the theater for hooliganism with Frank Costello. In 1916, he spent six months in prison for dealing heroin. Them, he was meant to join the military in 1917. He deliberately infected himself with chlamydia, a contagious sexually transmitted infection. A mass shooting with Lansky was spectacular. In 1925, there was a kidnapping. He was sent to jail for 30 to 50 years in 1936; however, he enjoyed preferential treatment, being able to maintain his relationships and business even from prison. Roosevelt even worked with him in secret as he was able to cash huge donations. This Kosher Nostra mafia was allowed to build its luxury brothel on Varadero beach in Cuba; in Las Vegas, almost all of the grand hotels belong to them. Luciano was released to capitalize on his contacts in Sicily. The official release took place in 1946 following the war in Naples, so 10 years after being incarcerated for 50 years. There is an interesting novel about his life written by Jack Higgins, titled "Luciano".

His wording when he was summoned to a court hearing is also famous. He warned his friend Franklin Roosevelt, "Frankly, my witnesses are prostitutes, madams, and heels".

The conclusion regarding the participation of the mafia in the recapture of Sicily is that the mafia eliminated by Il Duce re-emerged with even greater influence than before.

Continuation of Antonio's contribution

He approved of John's remarks and also pointed out that the Sicilian mafia experienced a genuine renaissance and even formed alliances with the Camorra and Cosa Nostra. He also noted that it is a characteristic of American politics to team up with criminals, even terrorists. It has been officially admitted that Osama Bin Laden was trained to be a terrorist by the CIA and supplied with money and weapons. At the time, albeit, he was going to be deployed against the Soviet Union, which was embroiled in conflicts with the warlords in Afghanistan.

IS in Syria

Antonio was also aware that the USA, which had illegally invaded Syria, ostensibly to fight IS, had actually trained IS by giving them weapons and financial support so that they could provide generous pay to soldiers from around the world. Therefore, young men, primarily from poor countries, North Africa and Tunisia in particular, flocked to join the fight in Syria because they would receive generous pay. Bashar Al-Assad did not suit the Americans; they wanted to get rid of him. But the imported war was passed off as a civil war in which the people wanted to win freedom and democracy.

Hillary Clinton

She also openly declared that she welcomes Islamic State (IS) because they are fighting Bashar Al-Assad. Netanyahu and his defense minister, Liebermann, even admitted that they are supporting IS financially and with technological weapons for the very same reason.

At this point, I had to make a point of my own. Our defense minister is of the opinion that it is important to continue the war in Syria. Even if this comes at the expense of the Syrian people to eliminate the dictator Assad, who "is killing his own people". If the American troops were to withdraw now, there is the danger that millions of Syrian refugees would return and rebuild their country. In this case, Assad would likely remain in power as it is feared that he will be elected by the Syrian people in a scheduled democratic election, something that is considered by informed insiders and experienced politicians to be very likely and which must be avoided under all circumstances. But why?

Antonio explains further

By no means annoyed by the continuing interruptions, Antonio continued his story. He reported that Taranto was captured between July 10th and August 17th, 1943. This city was chosen because it was barely fortified. The operation was known as Husky. In Syracuse, 470,000 German soldiers were standing under General Kesselring. A landing there would certainly not have succeeded.

The mafia's groundwork had also led to the Italian soldiers having no further interest in defending Sicily. In most of the coastal cities, the Allies could move in without a fight.

We did not want to get into the details of the invasion from Tunisia via Sicily. Under the code name "Operation Husky", every detail can be looked up in detail.

In any case, the failure of the Italian troops, indeed the refusal to fight by the Italian troops and their generals, was more than overt. It was all well prepared by the mafia. Even the intervening of Germany army troops under General Kesselring could no longer change anything. The superiority of the Allies at sea and, in particular, in the air was simply too great. An international army faced a German army that had shrunk to 60,000 soldiers. Yes, it even came to skirmishes between the Italians and the Germans. Antonio admitted quite openly: "My father, who was stationed on Sicily, deserted as well".

Badoglio

It was not long before a group around Badoglio succeeded in arresting the Italian leader, Il Duce. He was detained on Gran Sasso. It is the highest elevation in the Apennines.

Skorzeny

The sensational release of Il Duce, met with worldwide expressions of shock, was carried out by Otto Skorzeny on September 12th, 1943. He landed on Gran Sasso in his Fieseler Storch plane, loaded Il Duce into his plane, and flew to Berlin with him. The details of this operation can be looked up under "Operation Oak".

Count Ciano

He is the son-in-law of Il Duce. He was also implicated in the plot against his father-in-law. He commanded the forces in the northern part of Italy. Il Duce now took control of commanding these remaining Italian forces and carried out combat operations against the Allied Forces. He put his son-in-law on trial. He was sentenced to death for high treason and shot.

Sarah Churchill

A parallel with Churchill suddenly occurred to me. He had a favorite daughter, Sarah. She was similar to her father in many ways. Above all, she shared his fondness for strong, alcoholic drinks. It was a common occurrence for her to appear in the early morning drunk in the gutter in one of the streets in

London's inner city. This was naturally embarrassing for the daughter of the sitting Prime Minister. Churchill complained about it often as well: "She simply does not understand though I keep saying to her over and over: 'Civilized people get hammered at home. Take me as an example. For breakfast I drink a bottle of Bordeaux, and I portion out small helpings from a flask of whisky throughout the day. And only in the evening in the club, once the sun has done down, does the real boozing begin.'"

Regular boozing

Nowadays, it is not necessarily known what this means. It was common in the old student societies to drink a jug of beer in one sip according to a strict ceremonial tradition. This was repeated as many times as needed until the winner of the pub was established. Since most were "smashed" after eight bottles of beer, they had to vomit. There was a room for this very purpose in which a row of combined lavatories and basins were installed alongside one another. Two hand grips for holding made sure that one maintained a firm posture while retching.

Churchill's regular boozing followed the Russian example. A row of club members stood at a long table opposite the same number of waiters, who constantly refilled the empty goblets, while the drinking session carried on all fours under the table. Once one's original place had been taken up again, there was a new command. The goblet would be emptied in one gulp. The victor was the last one still in the position to take up their place at the table.

Churchill's son-in-law

Churchill blamed his son-in-law for his daughter's wrongdoings. He was dependent on drugs and had a very bad influence on lovely Sarah. When Churchill learned from the press that Mussolini had had his son-in-law executed, he held him up as a role model to his son-in-law. He said to him: "You see, that's the way it's done. I would gladly do the same as Benito and just kill you."

He was not lost for an answer. "You'd better watch out! If your admiration for Mussolini becomes public, you will very quickly be denounced as a fascist."

Monte Cassino

After this diversion, Antonio could continue. He explained that Monte Cassino is a 516-meter high mountain, right by the sea, a gigantic boulder. It was a huge obstacle for the Allied troops on their way to Rome. The battles with the heaviest losses of the entire war happened at Monte Cassino.

Benedict of Nursia

In 600 AD, Benedict of Nursia founded the first Christian monastery on this massive rock. Previously there were no monks in Christianity.

What's also interesting is that Islam formed around the same time in Mecca and Medina and developed into a world religion. The massive monastery complex of Monte Cassino, formed here over a thousand years, was one of the greatest holy sites of Christianity. In order that this significant site of humanity's cultural heritage not be damaged by hostilities, the Germans established a quiet zone in the one-kilometer area surrounding the monastery. The Pope confirmed to the English and the Americans that there were actually no military stationed in this area, so that the Allies could not think it was just a German strategy to gain advantages through.

Bombing

Admittedly, Churchill and Eisenhower did not care about this: 230 planes dropped thousands of tons of bombs on this monastery. All 400 Benedictine monks inside were killed as were 900 women and children who had sought refuge in the monastery because they hoped that they would be safe there from hostilities in the surrounding area. The monastery was totally destroyed, right down to its foundations.

Rescue of artistic treasures

General Kesselring, who had long suspected that Churchill would not recoil from the destruction of priceless cultural sites, had taken the most important artistic treasures from this monastery to safety before its devastation: paintings by Leonardo, Titian, the hoard of gold, chalices, monstrances...
He took them to Rome on heavy goods vehicles where they were stored at Castel Sant'Angelo. Churchill raged. No fuel for war vehicles and this idiotic general was using it to transport this useless junk. He must be court-martialed and shot.

Roosevelt's reaction

The total destruction of this 1,400-year-old holy site of Christianity was sold by Roosevelt to the American public in the following way: "We have destroyed the Germans' master control room". That is to say, in the ruins of the monastery, a battered Nazi-issued public radio had been found. The so-called people's radio was the radio of the poor people who could not afford a branded radio.

International battle

After the destruction of the monastery, the entire area was of course incorporated into the combat area by the Germans.

They withstood the American onslaught; they withstood the onslaught by the English too. The Canadians could not take Monte Cassino either. It was now down to the Poles, who were known to be particularly close to the Catholic Church. They were told that the Germans were going to capture the Pope in Rome, so the route to Rome would have to be fought as quickly as possible in order to save the Pope in Rome. The Poles did then actually succeed in capturing the top of the mountain with very heavy losses. The Polish cemetery at the foot of the mountain still bears witness to the numerous victims of the Polish exile army.

Sikorski

This situation is particularly infamous because it was around this time that Churchill's move to murder the Polish government-in-exile was taken. The advancing Germans in the Russian campaign discovered Katyn, where Stalin had had 30,000 Polish officers and many members of the upper class murdered at the beginning of the war. Sikorski and the members of the government wanted to bring this issue to light. They were flying over Gibraltar and wanted to continue on to request an investigation by the Red Cross. Churchill could not allow this because he did not want to anger his ally Stalin. Therefore, the pilot was ordered to let the plane crash into the sea. He was allowed to rescue himself with the parachute. Apart from him, none of the plane's passengers survived.

Class war

Churchill knew well that the class warrior Stalin eliminated the upper class whenever he had the chance to do so. Needless to say, he also knew that this was the case in Katyn regarding the occupation of eastern Polish areas by Stalin. Officially, nonetheless, he could not admit that he was cooperating with an ally like this. The Polish public, at least, would not have accepted this.

An unhealed wound

To this day, Katyn remains an open wound between Poland and Russia. Despite the acknowledgement of guilt by Putin and the willingness to commemorate the day together with the Polish government, this was rejected by the Poles. The entire government delegation wanted to commemorate the massacre a day later, alone, without the presence of the Russians. The unbelievable catastrophe, then, was that the plane carrying the official government delegation crashed. The President, all of the Ministers, the Secretary of State.. 90 people, without exception, lost their lives as a result. Kaczynski, the twin brother of the President, blamed the Russian government for the crash.

Battle for Rome

After the fall of Monte Cassino, the route to Rome stood open. Because Rome, the eternal city, is a cultural gem of humanity of the highest order, none of its artistic treasures were meant to be destroyed. It was therefore declared an open city, which meant that no soldiers at all were stationed in the city. When a city is to be fought over, it is declared a fortress. This categorically did not happen in the case of Rome.

Burning of Rome

Roosevelt, who had little knowledge of history, did however know that Emperor Nero was famous because of the burning of Rome. He wanted to become as famous as Nero and his name to go down in the history of humankind as a result of the total destruction of Rome. This was trumpeted around the world as propaganda, so that the Pope had to intervene to prevent this crime.

Exchange of letters

A long exchange of letters between him and Roosevelt followed, in which the Pope described the exceptional nature of the Vatican collections. This however no longer piqued Roosevelt's curiosity because the greater the losses as a result of the destruction, the more famous his name would become. An American journalist, who wanted to take the pictures of his life when the cupola of St. Peter's Basilica fell, rushed to the top floor of his hotel with a view of St. Peter's Basilica every time he heard the air raid sirens, pointing his camera at the basilica in the hope of being ready at the right moment.

Sister Pascalina

The Pope's housekeeper, a nun from Altötting, eavesdropped at the door when the American president's delegate wanted to blackmail the Pope. He explained that all of Rome would lie in ruins if the Pope would not excommunicate all of the Catholics in the German army. At that, the resolute sister could no longer hold back. She wrenched open the door and said to the American diplomat: "You will leave the presence chamber immediately. It is time for lunch. His Holiness is in very weak health. He urgently requires a consommé."

Scandal

This was understandably a scandal of the highest order. The Pope had to disown the sister. She was no longer allowed to be his housekeeper. Caricatures appeared in the papers in London and New York. They depicted the German nun sitting on the papal throne with Pope Pius kissing her sandals. This story also made the rounds in Italy. There they spoke of *papezza tedesca*, the German female pope.

Broadcasting station

There is a broadcasting station in the Vatican. In dire need, the Pope took refuge there. He spoke to Roosevelt in this broadcast and stated: "I have saved 5,000 Jews from deportation to concentration camps and have hidden them in the Vatican and in the churches in Rome. If you are now to raze Rome to the ground, do you want these 5,000 Jews to die too? Do you want people to say later that you supported the Holocaust with 5,000 victims?"

Roosevelt knew, of course, that these Jews were hidden in churches and monasteries. Their deaths would not have amounted to much for him. But if it now became public that he would willingly accept these deaths – that was something he could not risk.

Destruction of the broadcasting station

Roosevelt had raged and he had ordered the immediate destruction of the broadcasting station in the Vatican gardens. The losses were tremendous. Many Vatican buildings were affected, as was the side wall of St. Peter's Basilica. Shortly after the end of the war, there was an entire series of postcards which documented the damage. Today, every memory of that has been obliterated. The attack was officially attributed to the German Luftwaffe who allegedly wanted to prevent the Pope having another opportunity to extend his feelers in the direction of America.

Roosevelt's dearest wish was not fulfilled. He did not go down in history. The one thing people tend to know about him is that, against statute and law, he became president four times. The fourth period in the office, nevertheless, only lasted a few weeks. During a sitting for a painting, which would preserve him in the pose of Abraham Lincoln for eternity, death came for him.

Frascati

The bomber squadrons and their bomb loads which were ready and waiting to destroy Rome were not allowed to be withdrawn without taking any action. For this reason, Churchill ordered them to bomb Frascati at least. This is a gorgeous town, 80 km south of Rome, where the wealthy Romans retreated for the summer even in Caesar's time because pleasant, cool sea breezes make the summer heat more manageable. This is where the affluent Roman Senators had their country houses and pleasure gardens. During the Renaissance, the highest ecclesiastical princes and bishops lived in magnificent palaces in Frascati. It is a place that counts among Italy's most famous relics of antiquity. It is also known for its excellent wine; the dry white wine is particularly prized. 1,000 of the 10,000 residents were killed. A German off-road vehicle, which just happened to be on the move, also got caught up in the hail of bombs. Its driver and a passenger were killed. So, Churchill could announce to the press: "We have succeeded in destroying the most important supply line of the Germans".

Invasion of Rome

The Allies were actually able to march into Rome peacefully, without a single shot being fired. With this, the war in Italy was basically over. Only a few rearguard battles still took place. It was not long until the Allied Troops were in Milan.

Hemingway in Milan

Hemingway, the greatest writer of the time, had initially begun his participation in the war with the Internationals in Spain.

Now he had joined the Allied Troops in Italy and marched with them into Milan. It is interesting what interests an American in such a venerable, European city of culture. He searched in vain for a long time, but was finally successful in finding a shop where he could buy wild game. Deer, wild boar, or European hare. He, the big game hunter, in the world-famous film "Snow on Kilimanjaro" or as a hunter in American or European forests, is only interested in one thing: hunting and battle. Life as a battle. Struggle for struggle's sake. This is the motto of the former epoch. Hitler also gave his book the title "Mein Kampf" (My Struggle). The strongest in the population survive. This is the belief of social Darwinism. Instead of "people" or "nation", Churchill used the term "the race". He was convinced that the most noble and capable race – to which he himself belonged – was in fact the Jewish race. His mother was an American Jew.

Castel Gandolfo

The Pope's summer residence. Churchill and Roosevelt had learned from their diplomats in the Vatican that the Pope holed up there. As Freemasons of the 33rd degree, their top priority was eradicating Christianity. With the destruction of Monte Cassino, they had already achieved a modest initial success. The big strike with the destruction of the Vatican and Rome was still denied to them because Jews there would have been affected by it. The Pope, however, as the representative of Christ on Earth could easily be preyed upon in Castel Gandolfo. Therefore, they began to carpet the extensive castle complex with bombs. It was lunchtime and kind-hearted sisters in the inner courtyard were focused on serving hungry, fleeing mothers and their children with soup from a large vat. A total of 1,600 mothers and their children had sought refuge from the war operations in the surrounding area in Castel Gandolfo. They hoped that would be safe there and escape with their lives. Far from it. Though the Pope was not actually hit, more than 1,000 mothers and their children were killed. They were all standing in the inner courtyard for the food distribution when the bombs fell into the courtyard. It was a partial victory for Churchill. At the very least the belief that the Catholic Church could offer protection had been rocked by this. The incident was kept quiet by the press. On request, they were to say: "It is possible that a few stray bullets hit Castel Gandolfo."

Recollection

I must confess that from the moment when we turned to the capture of the Monte Cassino monastery, everything was so all over the place that I could no longer quite pinpoint who was explaining what. Miroslav and Mila likely spoke of the passages related to Katyn and the fate of the Poles with their government-in-exile. John explained the story about Roosevelt and his involvement with the mafia and Hemingway. Lizzy was astonishingly well-acquainted with the events concerning the Pope. Antonio contributed the actual war events in Italy.

Lesson

In short, this absolute chaos cannot simply be left as is, especially as it likely concerns unconceivable crimes. What is really true and what is simply false reporting must be brought to light. Actually, that's an ideal template for a history lesson at academic high schools.

Digital lesson

In German schools, the use of iPhones and tablets should be encouraged. Under the supervision of a trained teachers, students interested in history can be taught how to verify which of these stories about Monte Cassino, Frascati, and Castel Gandolfo are true, and which are fake news. The students could choose from various projects:

Is the exchange of letters between Roosevelt and the Pope about the planned bombing of Rome and the Vatican still able to be found?
Is there information about the aerial attack on Frascati and the circumstances behind it?
Which sources can be found about the battle for Monte Cassino?
Does the film "The Green Devils of Monte Cassino" really depict the events true to reality?
Who ordered the bombardment of Castel Gandolfo?
What is the evidence of the destruction of the broadcasting station in the Vatican gardens?
What is known about Sister Pasqualina from Alttötting?

Criteria

The teachers should advise the students on how they can differentiate serious reporting from fake news. In this respect, such a lesson would not be merely a history lesson but more general an instruction for how to interact with the media. It can however be assumed that there is also truthful reporting on the internet.

Mussolini's end

Churchill had joined the Italian campaign. He, who had so often been ill, really came alive during the events of the war. Blood and thunder revived his spirits. When nothing happened, he was afflicted by depression so severe that he even had hallucinations. A black dog haunted him, as big as a calf. He called him Black Dog. It was so bad that he had to seek psychiatric help.

Charlie Chaplin

Against this background, he became acquainted with Charlie Chaplin, who also suffered from severe depression. Both had the same psychiatrist and for that reason they met several times. During a stroll on the beach, on the occasion of a big party in Hollywood, they became friends. It was there that Churchill urged his friend to make a film about their great common enemy, Adolf Hitler. Chaplin was, like Churchill, a Jew and Hitler was, of course, the biggest opponent of the global, international finance Jewry.

The Great Dictator

So, the film "The Great Dictator" was made. At that time, nothing of the atrocities that made Hitler alone into the greatest monster in all of world history could yet be reported, but the thought was that he should at least be made into the biggest laughing stock in the world to the derision and laughter of the public. Chaplin managed that with this film.

General astonishment

This story of friendship between the great comic and the great politician was met with wide astonishment. It was contributed by Douglas. Apart from Lizzy and John, nobody had heard of it. Houston was, however, then able to share that both had been constantly threatened by the acute threat of suicide for their entire lives. And, what's more, another parallel then occurred to him, a parallel with the most significant work of German literature: "Faust".

Suicide and a deal with the devil (Faustian pact)
He reported:
"Goethe's most peculiar work begins with epic, wide-reaching passages all of which culminate with Dr. Faustus wishing to

celebrate his suicide with almost religious fervor. And it ends with him making a pact with the devil instead."

Black Dog

During the Easter walk that he took after the chiming of the Easter bells stopped him from committing suicide – he had already raised the cup containing the deadly poison to his lips and started to drink – a black poodle joined him and refused to be dismissed. In the scholar's narrow study, however, unbelievable things happen with the dog.

"Is it shade? Is it reality?
How is my poodle long and wide
What a ghost I have brought into the house,
it already looks like a camel."

It had already taken on the proportions of Churchill's Black Dog. And when Dr. Faust then conjures up the monster, since:

"It swells like an elephant,
It fills the room completely."

Only the threat to conjure it with the sign of the Trinity, the strongest sign that the magician Faust possesses, prompts the black monster to reveal his identity. Mephistopheles, the devil, emerges.

"So that was the poodle's core."

Faust now recognizes this. And it is with this devil that Faust now agrees a deal. He sells his soul and signs it in his own blood: "Blood is a juice with curious properties."

Satanists

It is well-established that Churchill was a practicing Satanist. It is also becoming more and more well-established that all Freemasons of the 30th degree, as well as the Illuminati, celebrate Satanic cults. The Bohemian Grove in California where all of the luminaries of politics gather is well-known; Kissinger, American presidents, everybody who is anybody in the establishment.

Lucifer

He is the bringer of light, as his name suggests. His devotees are the enlightened, the Illuminati. He ushered in the Age of Enlightenment, the *siècle des lumières*. During the French Revolution, the Church and religion were abolished. Monks and the clergy were pursued and killed. In Notre Dame, in Paris, human reason was crowned as the monarch. Lucifer is the god of the world.

Freedom, equality, brotherhood

Noble slogans were meant to obscure the truth of these aims. The ideals of the French Revolution were:

1. **Freedom** from all morality, from all statues, from all law, from any sense of shame, from all previous attitudes to morality

2. **Equality**. Abolition of every hierarchy, every rank, every grandeur. Everyone should be absolutely equal in their lack of rights, worthlessness as human material for medical experiments, as a store for organs that can also be transferred under the name "organ donation", and as submissive cannon fodder

3. **Brotherhood**, in the sense of "And if you do not want to be my brother, I'll bash your skull in". In other words, everyone is damned to followership, with no right to their own wishes or opinion.

Protest

I had grown quite dizzy and among the others, too, awkward silence reigned. "What you have presented to us there, Houston, is worse than any conspiracy theory. You have lost your grip on the reins of your Pegasus and your imagination has run away with you again." This was my objection. Charles was even clearer: "Your interpretation of the French ideals of the Revolution, Houston, exceeds even the most extreme extremists in its radicalism".
If Houston had not been our friend, surely some of us would have left the room in protest. In any case, the wonderful Italian dishes we had enjoyed at the beginning of the evening were still sitting heavily in all of our stomachs.

Cynthia

She was the first to recover her voice: "Even though your depiction of Cerberus, the hound of hell, left us in a daze, your reading of the ideals of the revolution has completely shocked us. Nevertheless, we still want to hear from Antonio how the Italian campaign came to an end." Then we would all head home. It was already late.

End of the Italian campaign

For Antonio, the only one who had survived this catastrophic bad news almost laughing, had no problem with Cynthia's request. He was the sort of person who could not disturbed be disturbed anything. "*Laissez faire*" and "*dolce farniente*" were the name of his game. This allowed him to glide through life without a care instead of struggling for survival each daily. Better to watch and wait. This demeanor is also what makes the Italians so appealing and likeable. He began, therefore, to tell us quickly about the end of the war in Italy. With the entry of the Allies into Milan, the war was basically over. The last of Il Duce's scattered troops retreated into the mountains and valleys of the North Italian Alps, pursued by only a few isolated Communist guerillas.

Capture of Il Duce

Il Duce himself had put on the uniform of a German Wehrmacht corporal as a disguise and evidently wanted to escape over the Maloja Pass in order to find safety in Switzerland, when he, along with his last remaining loyalists, was recognized during a raid by Communist guerillas on Lake Como and taken prisoner.

Notification

Churchill, who had moved into Milan with the Allied Troops, heard of this capture through his informants in the secret service. He needed to relax somewhat, to recover, to recuperate from the strains of the campaign. He would go for a few days' relaxation on Lake Como.

Giulino di Mezzegra

He knew exactly where he needed to go "to relax", namely Giulino di Mezzegra, exactly where the communist guerillas had taken Il Duce and his companions prisoner. He made contact with them and wanted to persuade them to deliver Il Duce to him. But even despite payment of a large amount of dollars, they were not prepared to release the prisoners. They were extremely proud of having hunted him down.

Firing order

Nevertheless, Churchill had to prevent Mussolini coming before a court under all circumstances. The English government and Churchill himself were too strongly implicated in the build-up and financing of fascism in Italy. This could absolutely not be made public. No price was too high to ensure this. Therefore, he managed to convince the guerillas – with brutal threats and great promises – to shoot Il Duce and his comrades. He would have ordered that himself in order to avoid a court case.

The bodies

The body of Il Duce, his lover Clara Petacci, and his comrades were thrown onto a truck, which transported them to Milan. Churchill has envisaged a particular spectacle. They would be dumped in Piazzale Loreto so that the common people, who find enjoyment in such amusements, could defile their bodies.

16-minute short film

An amateur filmmaker captured what went on there at the time. The recording still exists. It shows how the entire people, men and women, trampled over the bodies. They trod on their faces with boots and shows, kicked their heads... Their enthusiasm is visible, it was such a pleasure for them.

Hanging

After Churchill gave the order for the defiled bodies to be hung up from their feet, for show and for the amusement of the people. A genuinely uplifting tragedy, an accurate reflection of the imaginative poet Churchill. Worthy of Shakespeare, his countryman. The moral of the story was personally delivered by him: It is a quotation, from Il Duce himself: "Everybody dies in character".

"And so it was."

With this, Antonio concluded his remarks. Awkward silence. Even the talk by lively Antonio left hopelessness in its wake. "The curtain's down and open to all questions", is how Brecht ended his pieces at the Schiffbauerdamm Theater in Berlin. But we could not really end this evening like this. Therefore, Houston added one final point. He said an ending with horror is nonetheless an ending and better than never-ending horror. At least the war in Italy was now finished.

Hitler's end

He had heard of the death of his friend and comrade in arms Mussolini and also how his body and those of his lover were released for defilement and the amusement of the people. He knew that Churchill had planned something similar for his own death. He was to be paraded past the cheering masses in a triumphal procession. He would be in a tiger cage belonging to the Sarrasani Circus, suspended by his hands and legs, across Broadway and Times Square in New York.

Burning

To avoid this, he ordered that he and Eva Braun should be covered in petrol after their suicides so that they could be burned beyond recognition. This happened two days after the events in Milan. Hitler wrote in his will on April 29th, 1945: "In addition, I do not want to fall into the hands of enemies who require a new spectacle arranged by Jews for the amusement of the hating masses".

A good ending

Unfortunately, I cannot offer you a conciliatory ending either, Houston said in his final speech. With the deaths of both dictators, the bloody war was over for the time being, even if it was immediately followed by the Cold War. This war raged most acrimoniously in Berlin where the separation of the city into four sectors led to endless confrontations.

Hope

The stories of world history, which first and foremost take London as their starting point, are not quite finished yet. The records of our friend Henry only arrived on the eighth day. The book will not remain as an octameron, though. The 9th and 10th days are still missing. A third part will complete the 10-day history, the Decameron. I invite you all to my house for the next literary evening. There we will discuss the hopeful steps towards a peaceful world, the founding of the UNO, and the creation of a united Europe, as Churchill declared in his famous Zurich speech. It is above all this speech in which "the villain" mutated into the form of light, the bearer of salvation and the savior of humanity.

Forecast

Every year in spring, in February, when the climate in London is not very cozy, we head to the Cote d'Azur together, as we have done for years. We enjoy the flower parade on Mardi Gras there in Nice and the lemon festival in Menton. We also hope to enjoy that together again next spring. Hereby, we end our ten-day history again where it started almost 70 years ago.

Goodbye

Houston promised to let us all know soon about the date for a meeting at his house. The good mood had by now returned among us all. Each of us chatted excitedly to our neighbor about the little everyday things of life. Antonio treated us all to a grappa and so ended the eighth evening in extremely high spirits.